# Like Eating a Stone

Atlas & Co.
*New York*

# Like Eating a Stone

## *Surviving the Past in Bosnia*

## *Wojciech Tochman*

Translated by Antonia Lloyd-Jones

Copyright © 2002 Wojciech Tochman
Translation © 2008 Antonia Lloyd-Jones

Interior design by Yoshiki Waterhouse
Typesetting by KPS

Atlas & Co. *Publishers*
15 West 26th Street, 2nd floor
New York, NY 10010
www.atlasandco.com

Distributed to the trade by W. W. Norton & Company

Printed in the United States

First published in the English translation by
Portobello Books Ltd. in 2008

First published in the original Polish by Wydawnictwo
Pogranicze, Sejny as *Jakbyś kamień jadła* in 2000–2003,
and "They Came Back" first published as "Wrócili" in 2003

Map designed by Jeff Edwards
Photographs by Jerzy Gumowski

Atlas & Company books may be purchased for educational,
business, or sales promotional use. For information, please
write to info@atlasandco.com

Library of Congress Cataloging-in-Publication Data is
available upon request

ISBN: 978-1-934633-14-4

13 12 11 10 09 08  2 3 4 5 6

When you look at such terrible misfortune, you become overwhelmingly aware that first of all you are a human being—that your nationality is secondary. Humanity unites us in misfortune, in experiencing it. If only people understood that.

—Tadeusz Mazowiecki
United Nations special rapporteur on the former Yugoslavia
**1995**

# *Contents*

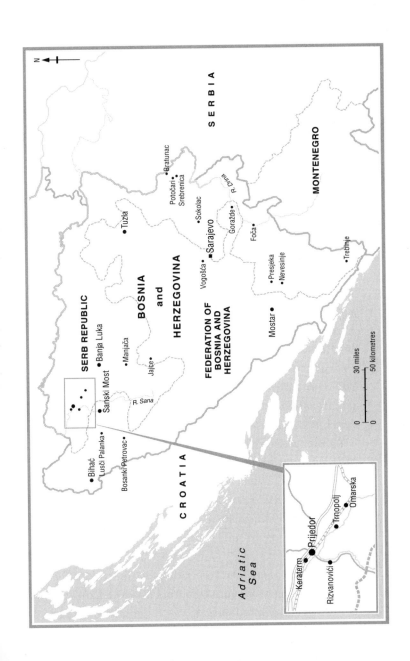

*In the mountains of Herzegovina, 2001*

Chapter 1

# *Frost*

It was the last day of 1992, the year in which the war began. We were bringing in aid for the besieged city. We drove into Bosnia from the south. Before dusk fell, we had already seen villages where no one was living anymore. The houses and places of worship had been razed to the ground. What had been done with the people?

We drove through Mostar, but we didn't see it. The city was like a forest: something seemed to be flickering behind a dark window, but we didn't know what it was. We were afraid to stop, afraid to enter this forest.

Just before Sarajevo, some Serbian soldiers stopped us. They were drunk. One moment they were laughing, the next moment they were shouting at us. That went on all night, until dawn. In the morning they confiscated part of our cargo and let us drive into the city. There was a frost.

In the city, amid houses and apartment blocks riddled with shell holes, we saw people—hungry and frightened. We were afraid too, because there was constant firing. We were looked after by Dragan L., son of a Croat woman and a Bosniak Serb, who had decided to stay behind in the besieged city. He was an excellent guide and looked after us well. He said that once it was all over, if he was still alive, he would escape abroad somewhere, because there would be no life for him here. I wonder where he is now.

In the hospital we talked to people who had lost arms, legs, and eyes. Sylvia, whose surname we didn't record, was the anesthesiologist there. "We need antibiotics, bandages, beds, crutches, prostheses, wheelchairs, and coffins," she said.

In the streets we also saw journalists—reporters, photographers, and cameramen. Writers and filmmakers were coming here, walking around in groups or on their own, talking in many languages. We saw particularly large numbers of them a year later, in February 1994, when they came in droves to see the marketplace at Markale, where in a matter of seconds a grenade had massacred dozens of people.

Thousands of news reports, feature articles, exhibitions, books, photo albums, and documentary and feature films have been produced on the war in Bosnia. But when the war ended (or, as some people think, was suspended for a while), the reporters packed up their cameras and headed off to other wars.

*Clothes laid out on the terracotta floor, Lucši Palanka, 2001*

## Chapter 2

# *Clothes*

The auditorium in the village cultural center is open once a week, on Thursdays. Anyone can come in and take a look, so people come not only from the local area, but from far away as well. They believe that this is where they will discover the truth. There is a stage in the auditorium but no seating for an audience. The clothes are laid out on the terracotta floor. They've already been sorted: this was found on the first person, that on the seventieth. Everything has been laundered to restore its color, then hung on a line to dry. The colored items of clothing are now lying close together side by side, though each one is by itself. There is rarely a complete outfit. For example, right by the entrance there is just a blue-and-white-striped T-shirt. It must have been worn by a well-built man, whereas someone skinny must have worn the one with "Montana" written on it. Further on there are some corduroy trousers, once white, now yellow. Who wore them? Under the window there's a single denim leg. Whose? Further on there's just a leather belt, just a pair of briefs, just one gym shoe, a single black sock. Next to each set of clothes (or rather rags) sits the empty paper bag they've been taken out of, and a sheet of paper with a large number printed on a computer.

There are letters too:

*B.* That means the clothes have a matching set of bones, a skull, and teeth. There is an entire *Body.*

*BP.* There is no complete set, but there are some bones. *B*ody *P*arts.

*A.* Clothing only, maybe some objects (*A*rtifacts). No bones.

All of this was dug up in the autumn of 1999 in nearby Kevljani (thus before each number we also have the letters *KV*). The mass grave there was a long one, stretching several hundred yards along the road (the roadside ditch was made deep enough in advance, and filled in afterward). Kevljani is near the town of Omarska, where in 1992 a concentration camp for Muslims was set up in a mine and completed its business that same year. Almost all the prisoners were men, though there were some women, most of whom survived.

The relatives of a missing person who they have reasons to believe ended up in Omarska eight years ago report to the auditorium. They come in and hold their noses, but they have no alternative; they cannot give up. They have come here to look, find, and bury. They believe that afterward they will feel relief and find peace.

They look around. Between one set of clothing and another there is a narrow aisle. To avoid disturbing anything with their shoes, they walk as if along a line. They bend over something. No one is sure; each of them moves on, stops, then moves on again. This goes on for half an hour, an hour, or three hours, as each person wishes.

There are rats running around in the hall.

A young couple carrying a seven-year-old girl are looking for their father, the little girl's grandfather. For a long while they stand over clothing *KV* 22 *B.*

A gray-haired lady in a navy-blue suit is bending over some other ragged pieces of clothing. She has been bending over the same outfit since morning. She keeps arranging it, as if she wanted it to look presentable. She straightens out the dark trousers, light shirt, and something that used to be a dark-red sweater. She caresses it all just as you would caress a person.

She is known as Mother Mejra.

**Body Bags**

The young people with the seven-year-old girl, who have spent such a long time near the stage looking at clothing *kv* 22 *b*, call over the person in charge of identification. She is an energetic white-haired woman in jeans. Her name is Ewa Elwira Klonowski.

Dr. Ewa Klonowski was born in 1946. By training an anthropologist, a member of the American Academy of Forensic Sciences, she is a wife and mother who emigrated from Poland during martial law. She used to live in Wrocław but now lives permanently in Reykjavík, Iceland. There she became a specialist in paternity inquiries, because she could not work in the field that fascinates her the most: bones.

"I love bones; bones speak to me. I can look at some bones and I know what illnesses the person had, how he walked, how he liked to sit. I can determine nationality by bones. A Muslim's femur is bent into a slight arc, because Muslims squat. Japanese have the same feature because they often kneel."

History has given Dr. Klonowski the chance to do some fascinating work in Bosnia and Herzegovina. The war and the end of the war have meant concentration camps, mass executions, mass graves, mass exhumations, and the need for identification.

Dr. Klonowski had herself inoculated against tetanus

and jaundice and packed her bags. Her husband and two teenage daughters saw her off at the airport.

She has been working in Bosnia since 1996, first for the International Criminal Tribunal for the former Yugoslavia at The Hague (the judges want to know who did the killing, how they did it and how many people were killed; they do not need to know the victims' names). Now, for Icelandic and American government money, she works for the Bosniak Commission on Missing Persons (for whom identification of the victims is the priority). Dr. Klonowski has dug up some two thousand bodies. She has fished them out of wells, recovered them from caves, and dug them out of rubbish dumps or from under piles of pig bones.

Now she is checking something in her papers, putting on her rubber gloves and going up onto the stage. The young woman and her husband (who is still carrying their daughter) are standing in front of it. Dr. Klonowski steps (cautiously, to avoid treading on anything) among some small, tightly sealed plastic bags. She is looking for the one with the number *KV 22 B.*

She finds the right bag, and opens it. She takes out an upper jawbone, a lower one with several teeth in it, and some loose teeth. She fits them into the right sockets and deftly assembles the entire jaw. She goes up to the edge of the stage and shows it to the family.

"Could this be your father?" she asks.

The young woman examines the jaw closely, and looks at her husband as if he might give her some advice. Their little daughter is holding her nose.

"Yes, that could be my father," says the woman quite calmly.

"OK," says Dr. Klonowski, packing the jaw back into the bag and returning it to its place. "Let's move on."

"On" means to the other end of the village (which is called Lušci Palanka), where there is a concrete barracks, once a workers' canteen.

A few months ago some large tables were set up in front of the barracks, and a hosepipe was brought over from the nearest farm. The locals gathered around the tables—men, women, and children. They watched as Dr. Klonowski sorted out the bones, determining sex and age, and packed them into body bags.

Now the body bags are lying on the ground in the dark barracks, waiting for someone to claim them. They are white plastic bags with zip fasteners—a bit like protective covers for men's suits but six and a half feet long.

We look for body bag *KV 22 B*. There it is, lying against the wall, right in the corner, under some others. Dr. Klonowski sets the ones on top to one side and pulls out the right one. She undoes the zipper. The little girl watches; no one moves a muscle. Dr. Klonowski is not surprised. She was surprised when she first started working in Bosnia four years ago.

"Why do you drag your children here?" she had asked.

"So they will remember." Everyone gave the same reply.

"Did your father have a problem with his hip?" asks the doctor, holding one part of a hip joint in her right hand, another in her left.

"Yes, he did have some trouble," says the young woman. "He had an operation."

"But did he walk like this?" asks the doctor, imitating someone waddling.

"No, I don't think so."

"This one definitely walked like that. You must find the hospital where your father had his operation. They might have some documents."

"All right. I'll come next Thursday."

"Then we'll take some blood from you. We'll compare your DNA with DNA from these bones. We'll be a hundred percent sure."

Now Dr. Klonowski has time for a break. We go back to the cultural center.

The gray-haired lady in the navy-blue suit whom we saw earlier leaves her preferred clothing unattended for a while. In the room next door she makes us some coffee.

"I am Mother Mejra," she introduces herself. "I come here every Thursday. I help Dr. Ewa, and I comfort the families."

### A Bath

Mejra Dautović, aged fifty-eight, used to live in Prijedor. That spring, the Serbs had herded the young Muslim men along the streets in front of them as a human shield to protect them from the local territorial defense force. Serbian flags were flown from the official buildings and stations. The Muslims were ordered to hang white sheets out of their windows, and to wear white armbands. Snipers took up positions in the housing blocks.

Today Prijedor is in the Serb Republic. There is no place there for Mother Mejra. She and her husband now live in Bosanski Petrovac, in a house that is Serbian, not their own.

We follow Mejra along the narrow aisles between the scraps of clothing. We stand over that set of clothes—the dark trousers, light shirt and something that used to be a dark-red sweater. Mother Mejra leans over to straighten a trouser leg. She stands up and tries to decide if it all looks reasonably presentable.

"This is Edvin," she says, as if introducing someone to us. "My son. The sex matches, and the age, and the height, and the teeth. But Dr. Ewa isn't completely sure. They haven't done our DNA tests yet. I had Edvin"—she leans over to adjust the trouser leg again—"and I had Edna. I know all about what happened to my Edna. Who beat her up, who raped her. The only thing I don't know is where that bus went. Where they took her from Omarska. Her clothes are nowhere to be found, not even a shoe, nothing."

For several years Mother Mejra has been traveling around the area, putting photographs of her children up on walls. She has even written a book about them. She is intent on finding any information at all that will lead her to the truth. She wants to find out three things: How did her children die? Who killed them? Where are their bones?

When Mother Mejra cries (she cries every day), she hides from her husband to avoid adding to his suffering. Uzeir is ill—on top of all this, he has had two strokes and says nothing for days at a time. Sometimes he just gets up and pummels his own head with his fists. He falls over, lies on his back, and shields his twisted face with his hands. He writhes, as if trying to avoid the next kick from an invisible tormentor, and gets kicked in the belly, hard, then in the chest, in the head, and covers his face again. There seems to be a second invisible torturer too. This one usually kicks Uzeir in the back and the behind. Uzeir jumps up, falls down, and bends, like a big letter *S*. He groans but suddenly stops and stands up on steady feet. He stares in disgust at something lying at his feet. He is no longer the terrified father who went to the Serbian police station to ask about his daughter's fate. Now Uzeir is standing over an invisible victim, in triumph. He's shouting incoherently. He's kicking something with satisfaction. He's brutal; he doesn't stop for a moment—he keeps kicking harder and harder.

"Calm down," Mejra tells her husband.

When the war broke out, their son Edvin was twenty-seven. He was a graduate of the electrical-engineering college. He knew English and German. He practiced karate and was a black belt. That spring he joined the Muslim territorial defense force, and toward the end of May he was one of a hundred soldiers who attempted to liberate Prijedor. Wounded in action, he died the next day. That is how witnesses tell the story.

But there is another version of Edvin's death. Other witnesses saw him in Omarska. They saw him being tortured in front of his sister. They saw his corpse being thrown onto a yellow truck on June 16. The truck drove off somewhere. Mother Mejra believes it went to Kevljani, to a roadside ditch that had deliberately been made deeper. After all, this is her son's clothing; the height, sex, age, and teeth all match.

Edvin's sister, Edna, was twenty-three. Jolly, lively, and direct, she worked selling industrial goods in a shop that her father set up for her on the ground floor of their house. She was doing extramural studies in education at Tuzla. At one time she wanted to become a model. "She had a figure like Barbie," wrote Mother Mejra in her book. With the money Edna earned she was planning to buy a horse and a house in a mountain clearing. She loved hiking in the mountains. She practiced judo and karate and was a good shot. So when the war broke out, she immediately went after her brother.

Toward the end of May she took part in the action to liberate Prijedor. She carried equipment, medicines, and dressings for the soldiers. She managed to get several of the wounded out. After the fighting she went home to her parents. Terrified, she hid with them in a small shed; they lived like that, next to their house, for several days.

"She asked me to heat her some water for a bath," wrote Mother Mejra. "The Muslim houses had no electricity, so I lit the stove. Allah the Merciful wanted me to bathe my little girl one last time." Two militiamen drove up and took Edna away. She wanted to take a sweater for the journey, but they said she wouldn't need it. Uzeir immediately ran to the militia to ask about his daughter. He was beaten up and kicked.

He heard that they were taking Edna to Omarska.

Mother Mejra called Nebojša B. She knew him well.

Nebojša had been Edna's boyfriend, but now he was the chief investigator in Omarska.

He didn't come to the telephone when he heard who was calling.

According to the women who were taken away with Edna and survived, it was Nebojša B. who interrogated her most often.

Once he had finished, Edna was barely alive.

Today Nebojša B. lives in Prijedor and works for the police.

**The Bus**

Edna and some other women were taken to a barracks with a small loft where there was an interrogation room. For several days and nights the women heard the men being tortured downstairs.

Mother Mejra was still living in Prijedor. She went to see a close friend two streets away. She wanted to give her everything she had in exchange for her help.

"You are Serbian," said Mejra. "Do something so that Edna comes home."

But the friend had her own worries. For three days her husband, Slavko, had not come home. He had gone to Keraterm and disappeared. He was meant to come straight back. Now Mejra knows what happened to him: there was a prison camp at Keraterm too. In those few days, 250 people were murdered there.

Killing, washing blood off the walls, digging ditches—it all takes time.

That was why Slavko was away for so long. He only came back to Prijedor four days later.

He called Mejra.

"I stopped off in Omarska on the way," he said. "I saw Edna. She didn't look up or even acknowledge me. She was as frightened as a fawn. She looked bad. I went to the office to get them to release her. But it was no good. Edna had already been convicted for taking part in action against our troops."

Three days later, according to what Mother Mejra now knows, an announcement was made at the camp: several dozen people were going to be exchanged for Serbian prisoners. Edna was chosen, with one other woman and a lot of men. The whole camp envied them for the fact that soon they would be back with their families.

A friend helped Edna to get on the bus (which had a sign reading "student transport" on the windshield).

No one ever saw the bus again.

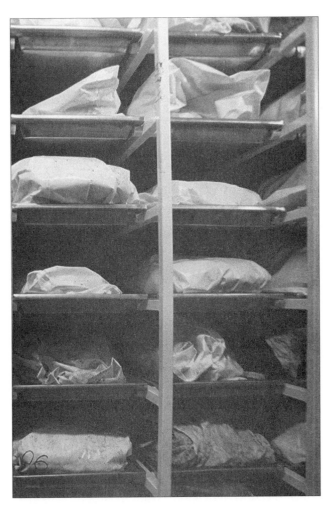

*Racks up to the roof, Tuzla, 2000*

**Chapter 3**

# *Chromosomes*

In Tuzla there is a salt mine, and there is a huge municipal cemetery. By the cemetery gate there is a funeral home, next to which there is a big hall built, apparently recently, out of metal. Outside the hall are some men in plastic overalls. The overalls have been excellently designed, with hoods.

These young men have found work here: they are pushing empty carts or wheelbarrows.

Behind the funeral home there is an entrance to a tunnel. The tunnel used to lead into the mine, but now it's a dead end, coming to a stop a hundred yards down. Inside, in the dim light, there are body bags on tiered bunks. They are wet because there's water dripping from overhead. The men drag out one muddied white bag at a time, throw it on a cart, and push the cart toward the new hall. Like full supermarket trolleys, the carts are hard to push, and the boys do not always make it around the corners.

Just as we arrived, a transfer of bodies was in progress.

The bones in the tunnel are probably those of the men who were last seen that July during a selection. They had gone missing. Later they were found and exhumed. They are all unidentified. They were usually found lying in so-called "secondary mass graves." Once an American satellite had spotted freshly disturbed earth, the murderers tried to erase the evidence by digging up the graves with mechanical diggers and burying what they dug up somewhere else (in rubbish dumps, for example). Many of the primary graves along the River Drina were probably destroyed in this way.

Now the anthropologists and forensic specialists are having problems because the bones from the secondary graves are harder to sort. It is more difficult to assemble an entire person (that is why most of them are marked *BP*). It is even harder to assemble the so-called surface bodies, the ones no one ever buried, that were left lying about on the ground, in the mountains surrounding the town. Time, rain, and animals have made the specialists' work harder.

From the bones collected in the forest it has been possible to count a total of 417 people—men, women, and children— because quite often whole families tried to escape across the mountains. If they were all killed, no one is looking for them; no one has filled in any search forms or provided so-called "ante-mortem information." They do not appear in the statistics. They will remain forgotten.

The hall in Tuzla is impressive. In the cold store, which takes up the greater part of the building, a computer maintains the correct temperature. Special racks have been built right up to the roof—lightweight metal structures with metal trays, each of which is six and a half feet long and has wheels on the underside. When one lot of men arrives with a body bag, others are already waiting with an empty tray set on a forklift truck. The truck is brightly colored and was definitely bought recently. The men transfer a white bag onto the tray, the forklift raises it and its contents to the right height, and the wheels allow it to be pushed into the right place. It all works like a good drawer.

Unfortunately, the designer didn't think it through completely—there are too few drawers, only 860. But there are already thirty-five hundred white bags. The local workmen have proved to be inventive: they roll up each bag like a sleeping bag (the bags can be rolled up because there are only a few pounds of bones packed loosely inside them) and put three people on each tray.

What will happen when the rest of the men are found? Several thousand men. Where will they be placed?

They'll have to make room by quickly identifying the bones that are lying on the trays and then burying them. The results so far have been unimpressive: only seventy-six bodies have been identified, and only because the victims had documents on them. (Very few people had papers in their pockets because most had thrown them away in fear.)

To increase the efficiency of the work, a catalog is soon to be published with photographs of the clothing. As in Lušci Palanka, it has already been sorted and laundered. Anyone will be able to look at the catalog. In the first volume, which is now being printed, it will be possible to examine 350 photographs.

Everything that is going on here (the construction of the hall and the identification work) is being financed by the International Commission on Missing Persons, established by President Clinton after the war ended in Yugoslavia. The commission will pay for laboratories to be built where specialists will test DNA. DNA is found in the chromosomes, and there are chromosomes in the nucleus of every cell of the human body.

This sort of laboratory is going to be set up in Tuzla, among other places. Relatives (children, siblings, and parents) who have filled in search forms will be summoned to give blood. From their blood cells the specialists will determine their DNA. The data collected will be entered into a computer.

They will also take DNA samples from the bones in the body bags, and these results will be entered into the database too. As half a person's chromosomes are identical to those of the mother, and half to those of the father, a specially written computer program will match the relatives with the right body-bag number. The whole process costs at most a hundred dollars per person. The world will pay for it.

DNA testing is something new in the history of war. So are body bags, computers, the Internet, computerized cold stores, forklift trucks, and trays on wheels. Apart from that, it has all happened before: prison camps, barracks, selections, ghettoes, hiding places, the sheltering of victims, armbands, piles of shoes left behind by victims of mass murder, hunger, looting, late-night knocks on doors, people disappearing from their homes, blood on the walls, the burning of farmsteads, burning barns with people inside, massacres of entire villages, besieged cities, human shields, the raping of women, the killing of educated people first, columns of refugees, mass executions, mass graves, mass exhumations, international tribunals, and people disappearing completely.

After the war in Bosnia almost twenty thousand Muslims were missing.

If anyone is found, there will be a funeral and there will be prayers, as required by the Koran.

### The Journey

It stinks on the bus because the women passengers

are smoking, but they aren't allowed to open the windows a single inch because there is frost on the glass and the heating isn't working. The women are wearing headscarves and long, heavy skirts, but even so they're shivering—not from cold, more likely from nerves. Maybe from fear, though they say their greatest fear is already behind them. They left it in the valley that day. As it is impossible to be more afraid than that, they have decided to go there, some of them for the second or even the third time.

We are driving out of Sarajevo, heading east. The road is steep, slippery, and full of potholes. Although it's already April, it is snowing. We have one hundred miles ahead of us, and we should reach our destination at noon.

Mubina Smajlović (aged thirty-six) is going for the first time. She has been working herself up to making this journey for a long time.

"I can't understand it," she told her mother five years ago, immediately after it happened. "It doesn't make sense."

"If we knew anything at all," she said two years ago, "maybe we'd feel a bit better."

"You can't live in two worlds," she said a year ago. "One foot in this one, and one in the other."

"Let's go there!" she suggested recently. "Let's go and see what it's like there."

"No," her mother said. "I'm never going there."

Mubina got up before dawn today. She kissed her sleeping sons, had a short conversation with her mother (who suffers from insomnia), and washed down some white pills with coffee (no breakfast, as no one here eats at that time of day). She put on a short raincoat and ran down seven flights of stairs (the lift in their block hasn't worked for years, and her mother hasn't been out of the house for months). She crossed the bridge leading to the bus station. She sat in the front seat, right next to the driver, to get a good view of the road. And what is alongside it.

If she had sat at the back she'd have been noticed at once, because of her beauty: she has sad, dark eyes, red hair (red dye hides the gray), a broad smile (she does smile occasionally), and wrinkles. She is slender, shapely, tall, and energetic, dressed in jeans with no headscarf. She makes a list of passengers: they are not young, not cheerful, and they don't have dyed hair. Before the return journey she will check to see if everyone is back on the bus.

Mubina doesn't betray any anxiety, but she could well be the most afraid of all the women. She doesn't know the fear they experienced five years ago. She wasn't there. She had left three years earlier, in April 1992.

That month the war began in Bosnia.

Mubina left with her parents and small sons, one four years old, the other four months.

"Come with us," she begged her husband, Hasan.

"Who will treat the animals if I'm not around?" he had asked. "I'll stay and take care of things. The situation will calm down, and then you can come home."

Today it is exactly eight years since the day Hasan said that to her.

Things have calmed down now.

Mubina is starting her return journey.

### Plums

The frost has gone from the windows now, the meadows are filled with flowers, and we're driving along the

Drina toward Bratunac. We pass villages Mubina has known since childhood. The last time she saw them was eight years ago. What she sees now looks different from how it looked then: there are heaps of rubble and the burned skeletons of houses, the plum trees are in blossom, and there are no people.

As soon as war broke out, Mubina, her sons, and her parents left for Belgrade.

"I'm going home," her father had announced once they were there.

"Stay here," the women had begged him.

"I'll keep an eye on everything, things will calm down, and then you can come back too."

"Stay here."

"I'm where I belong," he said when he telephoned from Bratunac. "I feel calm."

But the area wasn't calm at all. The next day, Mubina's father didn't pick up the phone.

Nor did her husband, not at home or at the veterinary clinic.

"What's going on?" thought Mubina anxiously. She called the neighbors.

"Yesterday your father came out in front of the house," the neighbor began. "He was standing in the street, having a look around."

"He's always done that," Mubina interrupted. "Every morning for decades. So tell me, what happened next?"

"He may have done it yesterday for the last time. Some Chetniks drove up. They asked his name, looked at a list and shoved him into their car. Later on they stopped by again but without your father. They took your Volkswagen; they had the keys."

To this day Mubina doesn't know what happened: who took her father and where?

"I must find his bones," she says, wiping her eyes, and she takes out a lipstick and opens a powder compact. We're driving into Bratunac.

Bratunac is on a broad plain, almost on the Drina. The river divides the Serb Republic from Serbia (Serbia is clearly visible from here). The town has nothing special to distinguish it: a few streets, a hotel with a fountain that's out of order (this is where the Serbian general Ratko Mladić humiliated the Dutch UN forces commander), a bank where Mubina used to work, two schools, some houses, a few blocks of apartments, and some people in the streets.

The people are standing and staring, but in Bosnia that's nothing special. Unemployment is running at sixty percent, and here it is even higher.

Bratunac has only one distinguishing feature: it is next to Srebrenica.

You only have to walk a few miles along the tarmac road directly south, passing some factory buildings in the village of Potočari, and you'll find the town in a narrow green valley. For the entire journey the women on the bus keep asserting that this area is unusually attractive and rich in minerals. The local waters have healing properties—they are so rich in iron that they're red—and are good for anemia.

Mubina doesn't want to go down to Srebrenica; she doesn't even glance in that direction.

That's where Hasan went.

## String

A few years ago, newspapers all over the world were writing about Srebrenica: most of the town's population were Muslims. When the war broke out in Bosnia, Muslims from the surrounding area joined up with them. In total, about thirty thousand of them gathered in this crowded little town, and as many again in the suburbs. The local Serbs had run off to their own people, though apparently no one had forced them to leave. Serbian forces surrounded the town and the suburbs, hemming them in, and held the place in their grip for the next three years. The United Nations declared Srebrenica a "safe zone," which was meant to provide a guarantee that nothing would happen to its citizens.

Every day, for three years, about thirty wounded were taken in at the local hospital. There was one surgeon working there. He amputated legs and arms with whatever he had—a razor and a sickle. There were no anesthetics and no antibiotics. For three years an average of five people died each day in Srebrenica. But there were also days when twenty died (not counting those who were killed there instantly).

The people had no cleaning agents, no medicines, and no salt. They ate grass, roots, hazel flowers, and bread made of ground-up corn cobs. This sort of bread is very hard to digest and causes severe stomach pain. Toward the end, they ate what NATO dropped for them from airplanes. But there was too little food from the sky, so whenever it fell, the hungry people drew knives and fought over it.

The end came on July 11, 1995.

The Bosniak defense withdrew from the suburbs after

being informed by the UN that in a short while NATO planes would fly in and bombard the Serb positions.

NATO flew in too late. The Serbs entered the city.

That day the women from our bus experienced the terror that Mubina doesn't know. She did not undergo the selection that was organized in the village of Potočari.

Zineta M. (aged forty-eight), who now lives in Vogošća just outside Sarajevo, did go through the selection. She hasn't come with us today, because since that July she has already been to her home three times. At the moment she hasn't the strength for a fourth visit.

That day, when Ratko Mladić's forces appeared on the edge of town, people were going to Potočari of their own accord. They were counting on the help of the Dutch soldiers who were stationed there. Zineta went, in a column of twenty thousand people, with her daughter (then eleven years old) and her older son (then twenty).

In Potočari the women and children were told to go to the right, the men to the left. Whether a boy was still a child or already a man was decided by a piece of string that was hung at a height of five feet (some say more, others say less). Any boy who was taller than that was taken away from his mother.

The Dutch looked on helplessly at what was happening.

"We called him Kiram," Zineta begins.

"Don't look at me like that, Mama," he had said as he was leaving. "They're not going to kill the whole lot of us."

"Leave me my brother," her daughter had shouted, but a Serb seized her and threw her among the women.

"I counted his steps as they tore him away from me," Zineta goes on. "One, two, ten, farther and farther away from me. I shouted and he turned around. Twenty paces, thirty, he was already almost at the factory building. There the Chetniks stopped him and told him to throw his bag to one side. The pile of luggage was about two stories high. Kiram looked at us again, then went into the building."

That day in Potočari it was unbearably hot and people had nothing to drink. Among the Serbs the women recognized neighbors and colleagues from school or work. Pupils recognized their teachers.

Finally, Gen. Ratko Mladić, commander of the entire army, appeared in Potočari. "I have come to explain to you that Srebrenica is Serbian," he told the women through a megaphone. "You don't have to be killed."

Seven thousand men were separated from the women and children (some speak of ten thousand, others of twelve thousand). The women's gold chains were torn off and their wedding rings removed. Some of the girls—the prettier ones—were taken away. They came back after a time and with the help of their neighbors got on some buses. All the women were put on buses or trucks. Zineta and her daughter only left Potočari the following day, just before eight in the evening. They didn't know where they were going or why. They were driven through Bratunac, Kravica, and Nova Kasaba, almost all the way to Kladanj. They disembarked after nightfall six miles from the front line.

"Go," they were told. "Go to your own people. Stay in the middle of the road."

There were people lying on the hard shoulder.

"We didn't even check if they were alive," says Zineta. "We were afraid and it was cold."

The women settled in tents at the airport near Tuzla. Some of them would leave their tents at night to lament.

A month later they heard on the local radio that in the area around Srebrenica an American satellite had photographed some large fields of freshly disturbed earth. At night the women went outside and howled.

Thirty-three days later, a thin, gray-haired, wrinkled man came and stood before Zineta. He had survived that many days in the forest. She didn't immediately recognize the man as her husband.

"Did the boys come home?" she asked about her sons.

That July day he and their younger son, Kemal, had decided to split up: the father would go northwest via the mountains, the son would go south. They had agreed that at least one of them must survive to look after the family. They had also promised each other not to be taken alive by the Serbs, and that in case of emergency they'd each carry a grenade attached to their belt.

Her husband had come home, but not Kemal, or the older boy, Kiram, who had remained at Potočari. Zineta had to keep an eye on her husband, because this made him want to kill himself. The women she had made friends with explained that even so her situation wasn't the worst it could be: her husband was alive, and so was her daughter.

And Kemal was alive too! He came back after wandering in the forest for forty-four days avoiding Serbian ambushes.

But what about Kiram?

Four months later, Zineta heard on the radio that the peace treaty had been signed at Dayton in America. It established that Bosnia and Herzegovina would include the Serb Republic to the north, south, and east (where Bratunac,

Potočari, and Srebrenica are located) and the Federation of Bosnia and Herzegovina to the south, in the middle, and to the west (including Sarajevo).

"They've given half the country to the Chetniks," Zineta told her husband. "A generous reward in exchange for our blood."

The following spring the women found out from the radio that teams from the Hague tribunal were working around Srebrenica.

Thirty-five hundred bodies had been found beneath the freshly disturbed earth. The radio said nothing about the remaining several thousand.

For all these reasons, Zineta is reluctantly traveling toward her old home, and Mubina doesn't want to walk around there.

Mubina doesn't know Zineta. They will soon meet—there will be important reasons for this to happen.

Now we're going to Mubina's parents' house. On our way into Bratunac, we saw that it is still standing.

### The Family Home

Mubina's family home is small and white with a tiled roof. This is where she was born, this is where she used to set off for school, and this is where she married Hasan the veterinarian. She spends a few minutes standing in front of the house, looking at it. She complains about the neglected garden and commends the good weather. That's how she hides her fear of what lies beyond the garden gate. Finally, she pushes it open and cautiously goes up the concrete steps.

There's a young woman in the doorway who is also very

frightened. It's not surprising; these days many people in Bosnia are afraid of unexpected, unfamiliar guests.

Before the war, the present resident of the house lived not far away in Kravica. Her house was burned down by Muslims from Srebrenica.

"They escaped over the mountains through the siege," Mubina explains. "They confiscated everything there was to eat from the Serbs. Most often flour. A sack of flour allowed a family to survive for some time."

"But they burned the houses too," stresses the new resident. "They killed the Serbs."

"Yes, they did," says Mubina, looking around the room. She looks at what is left of her parents' belongings. Not much, just part of a wall unit. Everything has been stolen, certainly before the young Serbian woman moved here from Kravica, before the politicians at Dayton established that after the Bosniak war everyone could return to their own homes—every refugee, everyone who'd been driven out. The Muslims—called Bosniaks at Dayton—who were sheltering in the Federation of Bosnia and Herzegovina can now return to their towns and villages in the Serb Republic. Mubina's mother, for example, could come to Bratunac and tell the young Serbian woman, "This is my house. Please leave." If the tenant refused to obey, Mubina's mother would have to ask for help from the local Serbian authorities.

No Muslim women are trying to go home to the Drina.

Mubina and her mother and children live in Sarajevo, in the Grbavica district, which during the siege of the capital was controlled by the Serbs. Mubina's apartment (on the seventh floor of a tower block with a fine view of the city) used to belong to some Serbs. According to the Dayton agreement, everyone can return to their own homes. The Serbs who have temporarily settled in the Serb Republic or anywhere else can reclaim their homes in the Federation of Bosnia and Herzegovina, and thus in Sarajevo too. A few are already trying. With the help of the Bosniak authorities, they are turning the illegitimate Muslim occupants out of their houses. Those evicted usually get another empty apartment belonging to a Serb, who might soon come back to claim his property.

The Serbs do not always return home to settle. They come back to collect their belongings and sell their homes. Anyone who has the money can buy them.

The young Serbian woman could go back to burned-down Kravica. There's a so-called reconstruction program in Bosnia. Any village or town announcing that it will take in all its prewar inhabitants can count on help to rebuild their houses. The West is helping.

In Bratunac no one even talks about it. No one expects any Muslim women to dare to come back.

No one says a word about the Muslim men, as if they never existed.

Three questions are never asked in today's Bosnia: How is your husband? How is your son? What did you do during the war?

"It's me," says Mubina to Dragan, her Serbian friend.

"You? Here?" Dragan's eyes widen with surprise. They know each other from the playground. He was the best man at her Muslim wedding and her father's business partner. Before the war they had a joint counter at the department store, trading in bathroom supplies. Now there's not enough money for the counter, so Dragan sells faucets and tiles from a nearby storehouse. That's where we run into him.

"It's me. Here." Mubina cautiously offers him her hand, not smiling. Dragan invites her inside, fetches some chairs, puts on the kettle, arranges the chairs, rinses some cups, gets out some saucers, and puts the cups on them. Then she runs out to the shop. He is sure to have understood that we haven't much time.

We wait five minutes, ten, fifteen. Finally he's back. He brings some Milka chocolate and a carton of Happy Day orange juice.

"Remember," he says, smiling at Mubina, "here in Bratunac we've always been known for our hospitality, haven't we?"

"How are you doing?" asks Mubina.

"The children are growing up. Jovanka's working. It's rare for a woman to have a job now."

"I know, I haven't got one. How's business?"

"The market's weak."

"People aren't building bathrooms in Sarajevo either. Too poor."

"How are the children?"

"They're growing up."

"And your mom?"

"She's alive."

Dragan gets up with a worried look on his face. Our time is up. Some customers have arrived.

Outside, another man is eyeing us carefully. He's staring at Mubina. He's standing in front of the greengrocer's (from the way he's behaving, he must be the owner) and waves at us.

"You've grown up," he says to Mubina.

"I've aged."

"I've eaten more dinners in your father's house than in my own," he tells Mubina in case she has forgotten.

"I know, you were good friends."

"And what good friends! But my child, there was nothing I could do."

"Nothing?"

"I stood here and watched them take him away."

"What happened doesn't matter. But where are my dad's bones?"

"Who knows?" says the man, lowering his voice.

"Mama and I want to bury him."

"I don't know anything."

"If there aren't any bones, we can't mourn. There's no way to get on with our lives."

"War is dreadful," says her father's friend. "But it has ended all right. We've been divided up; we live next to each other but not together. Your visit means time is healing the wounds. It's all right, all right now. We can meet for coffee, even do a bit of business, but in the evening everyone goes home to his own place."

## Antemortem Information

After his wife left, for some time Hasan went on treating the local animals. As usual, he would go out to help no matter what time it was. People respected him for his diligence, honesty, sense of humor, and optimism. For some time he went on living upstairs in the elegant house on the main street of Bratunac. It consisted of two rooms and a kitchen, and he and Mubina had moved in straight after their wedding. Mubina wanted to visit it today: go up the steps, open the door, sit in the living room, and lie on the floor. But she didn't have the strength and gave up the idea.

She doesn't know much about Hasan's death. She would like to know anything at all.

Apparently he was always being summoned by the militia. He went but came back. They would summon him again. This alarmed the Serbs among his neighbors, who organized a hiding place for him in the forest. He spent several days in it, and one night, when the opportunity arose, the neighbors helped him to get across into Srebrenica. A day, maybe two days later, all the Muslims remaining in Bratunac were taken out to the school sports ground, where the first selection took place: women to the left, men to the right.

In mid-May 1992 almost two thousand men were killed at the local school. This happened three years before the selection at Potočari.

Those who escaped to Srebrenica believed they were saved.

In Srebrenica Hasan went to live at his aunt's house with other men, including his father's brothers, his mother's brothers, and some distant relatives. During the three years of the siege, Mubina spoke to her husband by radio several times. He never said a word; he just told her to say something. So she told him she had escaped with her mother and the children from Belgrade to Ljubljana, that she was living in a student hostel turned into a refugee camp, and that the children were growing up.

On July 11, 1995, the day of the selection, Hasan the vet was not seen at Potočari. Like hundreds of other people he had decided to escape through the forest. He chose a route across Mount Buljim.

That is all Mubina knows.

At first she used to wait for news. Whenever she heard footsteps on the stairs she would run to the door, both there, in Ljubljana, and after the war, when she moved to Sarajevo. She often looked out of the window and waited for the mailman. Nowadays, to feed her children, she goes to the relevant office every month to collect her deceased husband's pension. She has registered him legally as deceased. (All the unemployed widows and mothers do this to survive.) She has also filled in the search forms: one relating to Hasan, another to her father. Their basic data (first name, surname, height, eye color, hair color, skull shape, past illnesses, missing teeth, and broken bones) is called in professional jargon "antemortem information." Mubina put the antemortem information in an envelope and sent it off to Tuzla.

For many months now she has been waiting for a summons.

## Mothers

Zineta M. is waiting for a summons to Tuzla too. For several years she has been living in Vogošća just outside Sarajevo. (Refugees from the towns on the Drina also live in Ilidža, Iljaš, and Hadžići.) The two rooms on the top floor into which she moved with her daughter, younger son, and husband were completely wrecked, like all the houses in Vogošća. During the war the town was located on the Serbian side. When the peace treaty was signed at Dayton, the Serbs began packing up everything they could. They took the faucets, toilet seats, baths, sinks, tiles, doors, thresholds, windows, curtain rods, parquet, sockets, and electrical outlets out of the apartments. From a nearby factory they took the entire Volkswagen Golf production line; in the Yugoslav era, Golfs had been assembled here. On the other side of Sarajevo they took the engines, cables, and seats out of the Olympic ski lifts.

They couldn't take the walls. Zineta's family equipped the apartment modestly and is waiting for someone to knock at the door any day now to demand the return of his property.

"And then where will I go?" asks Zineta. "To Srebrenica? My former Serbian neighbor is living in my house. He's eating his dinner with my spoons, I saw him. He sleeps in our bed, on the same embroidered sheets Kiram used to sleep on."

Kiram, her older son, never returned from Potočari.

Zineta's husband and younger son came home because they chose to escape across the mountains. The younger son lived with the family for a while, then left for Holland in search of a job. Many young people leave. (In the past few years, 800,000 people have left Bosnia for a hundred different foreign countries.) Many of them say they will never come back.

Zineta's husband is out of work too. The money he gets from the state for his deceased son (345 Bosniak marks per month) pays for his dinner. He has large hands; he is big and strong and could do something with himself. For several years he has spent days on end sitting on a stool by the stove, and doesn't say anything at all. He doesn't try to find an occupation or make any decisions. Zineta has to do all the thinking.

Their daughter, who sits beside her father, never says

a word either. She doesn't chat with the neighbors, has nothing to say to her friends from the housing estate, and never speaks at school. Since that July she has hardly said a thing. She was eleven years old then, and still looks eleven now. Immobile, her face expressionless, she listens to the stories told by her mother and the neighbors.

Vogošća is a city of women. The unemployed women take pills to calm themselves down. They have set up various associations. Zineta is chairwoman of an organization called the Mothers of Srebrenica. The group even has its own Web site, the design of which was paid for by a Western organization. Once a month the association organizes demonstrations at which the women ask:

"Where are our sons?"

"How can you tell us to go back there?"

"How are we to work the land on our own?"

"What Serb will give us work?"

"How can we allow our children to be taught by teachers who are murderers?"

"Who will our daughters marry there?"

"We want to go home," say the Mothers of Srebrenica, "but not the way it was decided at Dayton. Our home is Bosnia, not the Serb Republic. We'll go back when our Bosniak troops are standing on the Drina."

Most of the time, however, the mothers carry on with everyday life in Vogošća. They visit each other in the morning (and a second time in the afternoon) to talk about what's going to happen: they are sure to be evicted from their apartments. And they talk about what has already happened. Zineta's close neighbor, who is no longer young, had a husband, two brothers, and four sons. Fortunately, she also had a daughter—the only one who's left. The daughter is clever and well-read and would like to study, but the mother hasn't the money for that. Without paying a bribe the girl has no chance of getting into a good school.

The neighbor from the block next door had three sons, aged nineteen, seventeen, and fifteen. She also had a father, brothers, and a husband. She did not have any daughters. Now every morning she wakes up regretting that a new day has dawned. She is forty years old.

The neighbor from the ground floor had two sons and would like to bury them. That is all she dreams of. She would like their graves to be in Potočari. But first she has to find their bones, and her husband's too. A cemetery should be set up in Potočari, and a memorial, so no one ever forgets what the Serbs did to the Muslims. Meanwhile, the local Serbs want to build not a Muslim cemetery, but a large Orthodox church. That is what the neighbor women are saying.

"They haven't got souls," says the first one.

"When I arrived in Srebrenica for the first time after it all happened," says the second, "someone called my name out in the street, but I didn't look around. I couldn't possibly talk to anyone there."

"I went to my house," says the mother of three sons. "Not too close, so I wouldn't be in the way. But even so, someone noticed me from the window. Someone else's children ran out of my house and picked up stones to throw at me."

"A woman opened the door to me wearing my dress," says the mother of the two sons she would like to bury. "She politely showed me the ground floor and the upstairs. She showed me around the way you show your apartment to someone who wants to buy it and doesn't know its layout.

In my younger son's bedroom she politely reminded me who won the war and whose town Srebrenica now is. I thanked her politely too, and left."

It was the same for Mubina, the vet's wife: she arrived in Bratunac, went to her parents' house, took a look around, had a chat, said thank you, and left.

"The vet's wife?" says Zineta's husband suddenly. "Was he called Hasan? Would his wife like to know how he died?"

## The Heat

Mubina doesn't want to go to Srebrenica.

There are houses there, apartment blocks, a school, and an Orthodox church on the hill. It's quiet and very hot.

The women don't take care of their appearance and the men don't bother to shave. Carelessly dressed, they sit outside their houses and stare.

They have already brought down wood for the winter from the surrounding forests, chopped it up, and stacked it in piles. That's all there was to do. Of fifteen thousand inhabitants in Srebrenica today, only one thousand have jobs, most of them in nearby Serbia. For a day's hard work they get about ten Deutschmarks (about seven U.S. dollars). Here there are no factories.

The factory buildings in Potočari stand empty.

Of the fifteen thousand inhabitants, eleven thousand are not locals. They are from Sarajevo, Vogošća, Iljaš, Donji Vakuf, Bugojno, and Glamoč. That is why most of them are unable to point out a single place where, five years ago, there was still a mosque standing. There used to be five white mosques in Srebrenica. Now there isn't a trace left of a single one, not a stone.

They sit and stare. They don't smile. They don't even feel like talking to each other. What would they talk about?

They could go somewhere, at least go and look at the bazaar. The bazaar consists of two stalls in the town center where they sell wilted lettuce and shriveled cucumbers.

No one goes there.

There are no people; it's quiet in the bazaar.

Nearby, some dogs are lolling about in the fierce sunshine, lying in the middle of a crossroads without any fear. Some small children are sitting in the roadway with no one looking after them. Some hens are poking about in the tarmac as if there's no danger.

There is no traffic.

On the school sports ground some older children are playing football—that is the only movement on the streets of Srebrenica.

Some teenage girls are sitting in an amusement arcade, but they're not playing any games. There's no money for the tokens.

Some of the people who are sitting and staring would like to go back to their prewar homes, now in the Federation of Bosnia and Herzegovina. Anyone whose conscience is clear can go back. That's what they say quietly, when no one is listening. But they're not going back. They explain that it's because of the politicians here. The local Serbian politicians warn them that going back means running away. And betrayal! No going back! You've got to stay here! And one day it'll be better...

## Daffodils

Mubina will soon meet Zineta's husband and find out how Hasan died.

For now she has one more house to see in Bratunac. The house overlooks the town; it's several stories high, made of red brick. It was built by Hasan the vet. When their second child was about to be born, he decided they would be too cramped in an apartment in the town center.

He put up walls and a roof. He put in doors and windows. He didn't have time to put in the floor.

Mubina has explained to her sons what happened to their father. They need to know, but she doesn't talk to them about it too often, or in their presence when widowed friends come around. That is why Mubina feels that what the women in Vogošća are doing is not fair—endlessly going on about Potočari in the presence of children. "They burden them with things they themselves are unable to bear," she says as we walk toward the brick house. Better that the children should forget. But is it possible to forget about anything in Vogošća? Vogošća is a ghetto to escape from. But there's nowhere to go.

We are outside the brick house. Inside there is a deaf-mute Serbian woman and her children; her husband isn't with them. She is scared; there is unlikely to be a conversation. In the garden, by the wall of the neighboring house (the ruins of Hasan's parents' house), Mubina picks daffodils.

"I planted them," she explains to the deaf-mute, and goes on picking. She picks the whole lot.

"We won't return to our homes," she says, as we walk back to the town center. "That's not why the Serbs provoked the war and purged us, town by town. If you've killed that many fathers, husbands, and sons, you don't want to see their widows coming back. You don't need us around to remind you who you are. Rambling on about going home is just one of the ways the outside world manipulates us. Look how well it has all turned out! Serbs, Muslims, and Croats living together again in multiethnic Bosnia. And our politicians keep repeating this, making the right noises to the outside world. They don't know what they're saying. They can't ever have been to Bratunac."

Sometimes Mubina's sons ask her for details. For example, how long would it take to walk across the mountains from Srebrenica to Sarajevo? Those one hundred miles. Because maybe Daddy's been walking for the past five years and is still on his way.

Soon Mubina will explain to them why they have to go to Tuzla and give blood. They might ask what DNA is. What are chromosomes? Why do we have half our chromosomes from Daddy and half from Mommy? Why do chromosomes last so long in bones?

Perhaps her sons will ask who that man is who keeps appearing at their apartment.

Mubina often thinks about a new husband and, in contrast to the women living in Vogošća, openly admits to having these thoughts: it's hard for a woman to rebuild a home alone; it's hard to bring up sons alone. And the Koran clearly says that a widow should marry again.

"But am I a widow?" asks Mubina, holding the bunch of daffodils. She counts the passengers. They are all on the bus, so we set off for Sarajevo. "It's a good thing I came. Because I saw—it's all clear now, there's nothing to wonder about. It's not my Bratunac any more."

## Happiness

Zineta's husband is waiting outside the apartment blocks in Vogošća.

"That July," he tells Mubina immediately after greeting her, "we all walked across the mountains."

"Did you go across Buljim?"

"Yes. There my younger son and I split up, so that at least one of us might survive."

"Yes, of course."

"We promised each other that neither of us would be taken alive. Do you know what the Serbs did to our men?"

"I know," says Mubina.

"They crucified them…"

"I know."

"The first day we walked without any trouble, but slowly. Hasan was with us. On the second day, somewhere above Kravica, we fell into a Serb ambush. The guys went crazy; they put grenades in their mouths. Bang, one-two, a dreadful massacre. Hasan did it differently from the others—he put the grenade to his belly. He curled up—like this, and that was it."

Now Zineta's husband is staring at the ground.

"What about you?" asks Mubina after a while. "How did you survive?"

"Under the corpses. But what sort of a life is this? My younger son has gone abroad, and the older one…"

"I know."

"Don't cry, Mubina. You be glad. I would be happy if I knew our Kiram had blown himself up with a grenade."

"Yes, it's good to know. The soul immediately feels less pain."

"Our Kiram stayed behind in Potočari. That's all I know. He went into the factory building."

## Dream

"A woman can live without a man," says Mubina the next day. "I'm going to live like that."

Once in a while Hasan visits her in her dreams, just as he did last night. He appeared for a moment and then went away. She wanted to run after him but couldn't take a single step.

*Cafés, noise, and crowds on the promenade, Sarajevo, 2002*

Chapter 4

# *The Widow*

The new Srpsko Sarajevo and Srpska Ilidža are administra-
tive districts that border the capital of the Federation of
Bosnia and Herzegovina.

Sarajevo is full of beggars, poverty, unemployment, and
problems, as everywhere in the former Yugoslavia. But there
are also smiles, music, cafés (hundreds of them!), noise, a
crowd on the promenade, and money: colorfully dressed
young people in techno clubs, students in lecture halls, smart
women out shopping, businessmen in good cars, foreigners
out for a walk (there are more than fifteen thousand of them
here), pensioners in the squares, and music lovers at concerts.
There are lovely bright apartment, huge supermarkets, good
(expensive) bookshops, several radio stations, German and
Turkish banks (with ATM's—a novelty), American films (the
latest), Scotch whisky, French cosmetics, Dutch chocolate,
and Chinese knick-knacks. There's an airport, traffic, and
fresh air.

Here—across the road but in the Serb Republic—there is
no cinema, theater, industry, or export, the effects of many
years of isolation from the world and a ban on trade with
Serbia, imposed during the war by the West. There is not even
a single proper shop. There are some second-rate colleges, but
people can't afford to study. There is unemployment (running
at eighty percent, among women almost a hundred, and no

benefits), a shadow economy, a black market, crime, corruption, and domestic violence (in Srpska Ilidža there have been ten killings within families recently, including the murder of children by their parents, husbands by their wives, fratricide, matricide, you name it). There are drugs, vodka, depression, miscarriages, divorces, suicides (most often a bullet to the head), conflicts between neighbors, aggression, and insanity. There is hunger, overcrowding, living in sheds or communal centers, children suffering from anemia, frequent infections, and bed-wetting. Toothless jaws, shoes full of holes, idleness, impotence, constant legal claims, and grievances against the Muslims, Europe, America, and their own Serb Republic government. Waiting for aid that isn't coming from anywhere. Though indirectly, all this is mentioned by Danilo Marković, head of the Social Aid Center in Srpska Ilidža.

"Who is to blame?" asks Marković. "The war. Who caused that war to happen to us here? The new world order. The Soviet Union was destroyed, and then our army. Good old Yugoslavia had the fourth-largest army in the world! We used to produce weapons; we were competition for the global arms industry. And they made us have a war, so we'd use those weapons up at home and need even more of them. The world turned us into savages, but we're normal people. We were just defending our homes, women, and children. I know what happened in Srebrenica. People were killed. But more Serbs were killed in Sarajevo than Muslims in Srebrenica. You must understand that, and not invent all that Dayton peace nonsense, mass graves, tribunals, all that sort of thing."

Most of the people here used to live in Sarajevo. Although they have not fled far, sometimes only a few hundred yards, they are refugees now.

Take Stojanka, for example, aged thirty-six, with two children. This is not the first time we have met: she and her husband used to live very close to the city center; their windows overlooked the mosque in the old town. She was a shop assistant and he was a factory worker. They were in the city when the siege began in 1992. After several months they decided to break through to their own people. (Many Serbs remained in Sarajevo to the end, and lived or died like everyone else.)

Today we're meeting again. Stojanka is walking along a Sarajevo street. It's already dark, but even so you can see she's as feminine, fragile, and delicate as she was then.

She doesn't live here now; she has just come for a quick visit.

She is a widow. When they escaped the siege and reached their own people, her husband was immediately taken into the army and told to fire on the city he had escaped from. He was killed by shrapnel. (Serbian men were usually killed at the front. Most Muslims were killed by a bullet in the back of the head or through the eye. Half as many Serbs as Muslims were killed in the war.)

For her deceased husband, Stojanka receives a hundred Bosniak marks per month from the Serb Republic (not enough for anything).

The children are growing up. Now they are living in someone else's house, a Muslim's house. The owner (he too escaped to his own people) recently registered the relevant documents to get his property back. Although the house is in the Serb Republic, the Muslim wants to live in it again.

Stojanka is threatened with eviction. She is crying: "They murdered so many of us! How can we live side by side after all that? How can we look each other in the eye? People aren't made of stone, are they? Where can I take the children now? To the barracks? And what on earth was the point of the war?"

The apartment with the view of the mosque was not Stojanka's property. She has nothing to reclaim.

Stojanka has nothing. She will go to the barracks. And if she can't stand it there, she'll go into a mental hospital.

They fled the city in fear of the Muslims. That's what she remembers.

She has a poor memory: she was afraid of the cold, of hunger, and of Serbian snipers. She could not have stood here, where we are standing, then. A sniper would have got her in the brain.

For three years the Serbs kept the city under siege; the water supply wasn't working; there was no gas or electricity. They shot people either between the eyes or en masse, entire lines of people waiting for water or bread.

Today it is hard to visit the city as if nothing ever happened, to sit in a café among the families of the victims, among people whom they still hate, from whom they ran away. It's hard to look each other in the eye, order coffee and smile, talk about the facts and determine what happened—and turn in the criminals.

Serbian men from around Sarajevo don't come to Sarajevo. They set out chairs by a potholed road in the Serb Republic. They sit, place their hands on their knees, and stare.

A few Serbs (mainly women) visit the city once dusk has fallen.

"Some of the Serb widows make a living on the Sarajevo streets in the evenings," says the head of the Social Aid Center, lowering his voice. "They have children to feed. It grieves us, but the Serb Republic cannot help them."

*They sit silently on benches, Sokolac, 2001*

Chapter 5

# The Suburbs

Now we are in Sokolac, in the Serb Republic, thirty miles east of Sarajevo. (It's on the road to Srebrenica.)

The afternoon sun is blazing and the trees are providing shade. People are lying about on their own, in pairs or in groups. They're almost invisible in the tall yellow grass. They're not moving. Most are lying on their bellies, faces to the ground, which may be more comfortable for them. They're not speaking.

The ones sitting on benches are silent too, poorly dressed, with greasy hair, teeth missing, shoes full of holes or bare feet. They sit close together, side by side, like at the cinema. A few hours ago they put their hands on their knees, and now they're just staring without moving at all.

There are trees, paths, and a few buildings (inside they stink of urine). There's a hole in the fence on one side of the park, and an open gate on the other.

Beyond the gate it's beautiful, some low hills and a large open space: the suburbs of Sokolac.

Beyond the hole in the fence there are some gray barracks, at least a dozen long wooden blocks. The washing is hanging out as if someone lives there, but there's no one in sight. We could go and check: maybe there's someone inside.

There's no one about; no one's coming out—better not.

They sit and watch: each one has his own personal film running.

But someone is shouting, or rather howling.

Someone else is laughing. He's looking in a small mirror.

Someone is banging his fists against his own skull.

Crying.

Staring goggle-eyed and sticking his tongue out.

Pissing on the grass.

Someone else is pissing his pants—it's trickling down his trouser legs.

Someone is masturbating.

Someone stands up from the bench—it's a woman of forty or more. She runs up to us, grabs me by the sleeve, and asks for a dinar, though they haven't had dinars here for years now. She says she's hungry. A man runs up too. Everyone here is hungry. An old woman comes up to say no one ever visits them, no one talks to them. They have no one.

Sometimes someone in a white tunic comes and gives them pills. Or shouts, pushes them around, and goes away. Life as usual in a mental hospital.

The sun is setting. It's cooler now. The people on the other side of the fence have just come out of the gray wooden barracks.

### Chefs

The women from the gray barracks—as we can see through the hole in the fence—have made afternoon coffee and served it to the men.

The men have sat down against the wooden walls, on the deck surrounding the buildings. They are drinking the coffee and will soon start to drink *rakia* (they must have made it themselves, because it's rare for anyone here to buy spirits).

Some children are kicking a ball around, playing basketball, and messing about.

The women are hanging out washing or feeding the pigs—they have a few pigsties here. Or they're eating. Most of the women are sitting.

As we pass through the hole in the fence—we want to ask them who they are—something strange happens: the men look first of all at us, then at each other, and get up. Now we can see how they're dressed: patched trousers, stretched, baggy vests, and worn-out shoes. There's a commotion. The ones drinking coffee outside their own doors slowly get up and go inside. The rest have a little farther to go (fifteen or twenty yards), so they can't hide their panic as easily: they scuttle off, startled like creatures in the forest, losing their shoes on the way. The cloud of smoke they have left behind goes on hanging in the air. The dog-ends they haven't had time to stamp out continue to smolder. Now we can hear them turning keys from inside the buildings.

What has frightened them? It's our camera. In the Serb Republic the men avoid being photographed and hide their faces. Whenever strangers appear, the Serbian men are nowhere to be seen; they simply evaporate. But you don't have to come all the way to the suburbs of Sokolac to discover this. You only have to switch on Serb Republic television (you can also get it in Sarajevo). The journalists occasionally visit Serbian villages and towns to see how people are doing. On screen, the women always do the complaining. There are no men. The local men are afraid that someone—a survivor—will recognize them and report them to the prosecutors at the International Criminal Tribunal, telling them here are the men who played football with Muslim skulls, or who forced Muslim men to bite off the testicles of other Muslim men.

The Serb men shudder to think the Muslim women will recognize them. They remember their faces, their stench, and their strength better than almost anyone.

Everyone in Bosnia knows that the International Criminal Tribunal at The Hague has two lists of criminals whom it is prosecuting: a public one and a secret one.

The public list includes Radovan Karadžić (leader of the local Serbs during the war in Bosnia), Ratko Mladić (who was then head of the army) and Slobodan Milošević (leader of Yugoslavia, deposed, arrested, and taken to The Hague; he will answer not only for crimes committed in Bosnia, but also Croatia and Kosovo[1]).

On the secret list, if it really does exist, are lots of Serbian men (and definitely some Croats, and a few Muslims too). Thousands, apparently. This is quite possible—to murder tens of thousands of people is no easy job.

Those men in the Serb Republic who agree to have a chat say that during the war they were chefs. And the ones from Serbia who came here to help them also did nothing but cook meals. They all keep repeating this, even to each other, and they've probably come to believe it.

But they are hiding: the windows of the gray barracks are slightly open, and the curtains are rippling.

---

1.  Slobodan Milošević died in March 2006.

The women offer us cups of coffee. We sit down on the deck.

They are Serbian refugees, from Sarajevo, Hadžići, and Rajlovac. Now there are Muslims living there. The Dayton Accords included these cities in the federation.

Here's a reminder: the Federation of Bosnia and Herzegovina and the Serb Republic are the two parts of today's Bosnia and Herzegovina. There are two police forces, two armies, two ministries of health, education, and finance. There are three societies: Serb, Muslim (Bosniak), and Croat. The United Nations high representative tries to oversee the whole thing. Order is maintained by soldiers from all over the world, the so-called Stability Forces (SFOR).

Order must be maintained in Bosnia and Herzegovina.

The women sit outside the barracks and complain that there's no work, no money, and nothing to eat.

They have high blood pressure, heart disease, diabetes, high cholesterol, swollen legs, bad dreams, and tattered nerves. Each of the men here has his own film. Someone shouts, someone howls. Someone laughs. Beats his fists against his own skull. Cries. How can you live in peace when there are constant arguments and fist and knife fights? Cut wounds, stab wounds—not just once, not just twice, the guys here have often cut each other up with knives. Or kicked an old woman black and blue. Ambulances, police. All because of the crowded accommodation (we cannot go inside to see) that they have to share with strangers. Someone puts his shoes in the wrong place, opens the window at the wrong time, or sneezes too loud, and at once there's a fight.

"Why did we have to have a war?" the women ask. "What did our sons get killed for?"

"For nothing," they answer. "For fear, homelessness, and bloodshed, for life in the barracks."

Before the war they had homes, with a full freezer in each one.

Now their cooking pots are empty. They died for empty cooking pots.

"Milošević betrayed us," they tell us. "He signed an agreement at Dayton in America consenting to the Serb Republic in Bosnia, but he had a different agreement with the people. We were supposed to end up in Serbia, united with our Serbian brothers. That was what we fought for, that was what our Karadžić fought for. And that's why he has to hide now."

The women clutch at their heads. "Now they're telling us to live with the Muslims again. But that's impossible." (The Dayton Accords say that each person has the right to go back to his prewar home, the Serbs to the federation and the Muslims to the Serb Republic. There will be no ethnically pure areas, as the Serbs wanted.)

The old women ask for Voltaren to rub on their aching joints, for pairs of spectacles, for something sweet, and for us to talk to them a bit, because no one ever visits them. They have no one.

### The Garage

In the suburbs of Sokolac the sun is just about to go down. The Serbian women are still sitting outside the gray barracks.

There is a man here too, Miša. He turned up a while ago and isn't trying to hide at all. We each drink a shot of *rakia*.

He tells us who he doesn't like, although we haven't asked him that: the Muslims, obviously; the British, because they're proud; the Americans, because they hate the Serbs; the Poles, because they joined NATO; and the Russians, because they are always betraying the Serbs.

Miša comes from Goražde. He lost his wife. She was on a bus that got blown up by a grenade.

We know about those incidents: when the city was under siege by the Serbs, the Muslims would hold Serbs hostage. In time they would allow the hostages to leave to join their own people.

The Serbian women and children got on buses, but before the Serbs reached their own side, the Muslims attacked the convoy. A hundred, maybe two hundred, people were killed (the data are not precise). Among them was Miša's wife.

They didn't have any children.

Miša is forty and has a house in Goražde that he cannot reclaim. Nowadays Goražde is Muslim. Miša cannot go into the federation, to the Muslim authorities. His old neighbors there will recognize him and will want to settle scores. So it's better not to move from here.

He has no work (he is a car mechanic) and is no longer even looking for any. He smiles when we ask where he gets the money for food. He won't say.

He doesn't live in the barracks. He couldn't stand sleeping in a stuffy room with old people snoring. He put up a windowless garage for himself. He papered the walls with pictures of naked women. That's where he sleeps.

He is looking for a new wife, though he knows no woman will come and live in his windowless garage—none of the ones sitting outside the barracks staring, anyway. They are twenty years old, with sad expressions. They ask us if we believe in Jesus.

Good, they'll talk to us. They can talk to Christians.

They haven't been anywhere for years. They haven't seen the sea, a big city, or other people. They're curious to know what it's like in Sarajevo (it's thirty miles from here). They'd love to go there, but they're afraid: of provocation on the streets, of beatings, of humiliation. Someone told them that's how Serbian women are treated there now.

We offer to take them to Sarajevo.

We'll sit in a café on Ferhadija (the city's main promenade). We'll have ice cream and drink cola, and we won't have any trouble. Let's help the Serbian girls from the suburbs of Sokolac change their view of Sarajevo.

But they refuse; they won't go. "The Muslims disgust us," they say. "They killed the Serbs; they drove us out of our homes. Now we have no homes. Sokolac isn't our home. It's just a barracks, a dump, a dead place. We've got to get away from here."

They want to go abroad (more than sixty percent of the young people here want to emigrate): to Australia, New Zealand, or America. They'd like to get married there. Not here. Who would they marry here? Miša?

Only one of them, Sveta, thinks differently: she wants to stay in the Serb Republic, because it's a Serbian woman's duty to get married and have a child here. Better a son; the nation needs sons. You can't live for money alone. Let Sveta be poor but at home, not among strangers. And maybe one day the Serb Republic will manage to join up with Serbia. One day it'll be better here.

Sveta is not curious to know what it's like in New

Zealand. She couldn't cope with people talking a different language.

Maybe she'll marry Miša, though he's twice her age. Sveta likes Miša: he's good-looking, and he doesn't drink too much. But he must have a house.

Miša knows the way to get a house and a happy family— war. Only war can change anything.

Miša cannot see any other path for himself. Now he's going for a walk; he likes to take a walk in the evenings. He goes through the hole in the fence.

*Today a Serbian girl lives in the house of Sabira and Huso, who were Muslims. Her parents have hung a picture of Radovan Karadžić on the wall. Nevesinje, 2001*

Chapter 6

# *Rocks*

On the steep road from Mostar to nowhere, in the stony mountains of Herzegovina, lies the little town of Nevesinje. Here in the town center the district governor, Boško Buha, runs his office: he is tall, thin, and suntanned.

"Welcome! Look how beautiful our Serbian land is."

"The Appendix"—that's what people call Governor Buha's district: sun-baked fields, empty roads, no traffic at all, no respite from the heat even in the afternoon. Rocks, boulders, and stones—it's empty and austere.

When Governor Buha was living in a completely different place (before 1992), the local Serbs (who were in the majority), the Muslims, and a handful of Croats used to produce car parts, pajamas, furniture, and health food. The land was for the most part state owned, but some people had their own bit of a field, so they'd take their produce to market in Mostar. They did their shopping there and sent their children to school there. The bus used to run to Mostar every forty minutes. But now there are no buses at all.

Formerly, about fourteen thousand people lived here. Now there are twenty thousand inhabitants; only fifteen hundred of them have jobs, and thirty-five hundred have no work at all.

The rest are children—who need to be fed—and pensioners.

If the Serb Republic is not late with the payment, the money for pensioners is enough to last a few days each month. No one knows how they live after that. Governor Buha has no idea—he prefers not to know.

We know how the pensioners survive—they sit. In the morning they place their hands on their knees and sit staring, without moving, until late afternoon, or right into the evening. They burn very few calories, so they don't have to eat much.

Half the people in Nevesinje are not locals, including Governor Buha.

They came in the spring of 1992 (which was when the war in Bosnia began), when they escaped from their own villages and towns after the Serbian authorities warned them that the Muslims (and eventually the Croats) would burn down their houses and butcher their children.

They managed to get to Nevesinje. The children have grown up, and they're still living here.

For example, in the second house along from the governor's office there are only women (at least that's how it looks). The house is big, with several stories and stairs on the outside. There is a family in each room. Three or four people in a space of thirty square feet: two sofa beds, a little table, a few cooking pots, and a portrait of Karadžić.

They complain that there's no running water. There's usually no water every other day.

The children are finishing primary school. How are children meant to get further education? Where?

Before the war they had a life.

They tell us that the owner of this house was Huso, a Muslim, who had a wife named Sabira. They went away to Sarajevo. Four years ago their daughter dropped in to retrieve a family photograph album.

"That spring," says Governor Buha, "the local Muslims left for Mostar, Konjic, Sarajevo, New York, and Sydney. They went to join their people. And the world declared that the Serbs were beasts, murdering Muslims."

It was summer, not spring. The governor and the present inhabitants of Huso and Sabira's house were already living in Nevesinje then. They must know what happened here.

Huso was a retired merchant, aged eighty. Sabira was a retired office worker (she was seventy). They worked hard, built the house, brought up their children, and were growing old quietly—until that July, in 1992. Until June, in fact, because the first murders of Muslims in Nevesinje began on June 10. First the rich ones were killed, then others at random. Huso must have known all about it, when in the first few days of July he spoke on the phone to his son, who was living in Sarajevo. He didn't want to worry his son, so he told him everything was all right here.

But nothing was all right. A few days later their Serbian neighbors (in the house next to the office) decided to make room for the Serbian homeless (today's tenants). They took Huso and Sabira out beyond the town.

Their bodies were exhumed in 1997 (with two uncles, their wives, and their sons). Sabira had money, a watch, and gold sewn into her clothing, so there was no problem with the identification. There was a funeral not far away, on the Muslim side. That was when Huso's daughter called in at Nevesinje and asked to have the family photo album back.

The tenants smiled as they handed over the album. The daughter took a quick look at her father's house and left.

*Jasna searches for her children, Borisavac Pit, 2001*

**Chapter 7**

# *The Mountains of Herzegovina*

It is July. Every morning before eight the same people gather at the Big Ben café in the eastern part of Mostar. The sun is already beating down. Thanks to the high walls of the neighboring buildings, the little square, where some small metal tables have been set out, is still managing to hide from the heat. The people in the café are smiling, chatting, and reading the papers; someone is making a phone call. It's plain to see they all know each other. They are all about forty, some a little older or a little younger. They are waiting for others to arrive. Others do arrive every so often, greet the people who are already there, and order coffee.

Dr. Ewa Klonowski is there, in heavy boots, denim shorts, a light shirt, and a straw hat.

Jasna Ploskić, aged thirty-nine, is there too, sitting with Sanja Mulać at a table. Sanja is head of the Mostar division of the Bosniak Commission on Missing Persons. Jasna is her deputy. They are sure to be talking about the place we are about to go to, and what we can expect to find there.

We're going into the mountains of Herzegovina. Sanja is giving the signal for departure, though the speleologists for whom we've been waiting for such a long time still haven't arrived from Sarajevo. And they won't—someone has messed up the arrangements, misunderstood, mixed up the dates, or failed to make the relevant decisions in time. In Bosnia it's all par for the course; no one is surprised.

We must go southeast from Mostar, into the Serb Republic.

On the way, in a Serbian village, we are joined by some Spanish SFOR soldiers, to protect us just in case. Now we are turning left off the main highway, down a white gravel road. We start to climb, braving the hairpin bends for at least six miles.

The mountain is huge and sparsely vegetated. The earth is scorched, there are large gray stones, and it's blazing hot.

On a flat mountain pasture the first trees come into sight. And a farm—someone lives here, though God knows what they live on.

An old woman comes out onto the road, raises a hand to shield her eyes from the sun, and stares.

She must be surprised to see a convoy of jeeps and trucks coming across her wilderness.

Maybe she was surprised nine years ago as well.

Did they come by day, like us, or did they hide their crimes in the dark?

We pass a barn and drive on, into the forest, into the shade.

### Neighbors

Before the year in which it all happened (1992), Jasna had completed her law studies, married Hasan (he had the same name as the husband of Mubina, who picked the daffodils), had a son (1987), reached the age of thirty, and had a daughter (1991). Hasan, an economist, was a successful man, with a solid income and a nice house.

His wife didn't have to work. "It'll be better for the children," they had said. "Small children need their mother full time."

A year, maybe six months before all that, Jasna had felt anxious: Serb reservists were firing in the air on the streets of Mostar, accosting people and insulting women.

The Ploskić family home, which belonged to Jasna's mother-in-law, was in Šehovina. That was the district of Mostar inhabited mostly by Serbs who had come from nearby Nevesinje (where the Muslim Hasan came from too).

In the spring her Serbian neighbors knocked on Jasna's door and asked to borrow some suitcases.

They escaped to Nevesinje after an oil tank blew up at a barracks in the northern suburbs.

It was April 4, and there was fear, confusion, and panic— the beginning of the war.

She lent the neighbors some suitcases.

"I will never forgive them," she says. "After all, they could have said, 'Jasna, don't go to Nevesinje. Nothing good will happen to you there.'"

Serbian troops occupied the city. Hasan, Jasna, little Amar, and little Aila, Hasan's brother, his wife, and their three children all went in a single car to an aunt who lived nearby.

There the Muslim and Croat women were getting ready to leave. They were to travel across the border with the children, to Croat refugee centers.

Any men who were fit to fight were not allowed to cross the border.

Jasna was ready for the journey.

She had forebodings that she would never see Hasan again. "I'm staying here," she said to him, and he gave in.

"People here just want to forget about that time," says Jasna. "The day I forget I'll go mad."

Today in the Herzegovina-Neretva Canton the search is on for approximately fifteen hundred people who went missing around that time, including about fifty Croats and a few Serbs.

Jasna and her husband decided to travel to the area around Nevesinje, where it was safer. Everyone there knew them—they were neighbors, after all.

They went to a village called Presjeka, to stay with her mother-in-law. They traveled across fields, forests, and mountains, a total of twenty-five miles—all of them, two couples and five children.

On the way they were stopped by some Serbian soldiers who checked their documents. The soldiers were polite and let them pass.

In Presjeka people were living as before: getting up, having a wash, and saying their prayers. The women spent their day watering the cattle and taking them out to pasture, cleaning their houses and preparing meals. The men were busy repairing machinery before the harvest (rye and wheat were cultivated here), complaining about the drought, and drinking coffee at the café. In Presjeka there was a café, a grocery, a school, and more than thirty one-story houses made of stone.

There was stone all around the place, and a few trees around the houses: plum, pear, and walnut trees. They weren't very big and didn't give proper shade, so during the day everyone used to hide away indoors. Inside it was pleasant; outside it was like a frying pan, scorching hot.

But in the evening it cooled down (the temperature difference between day and night here can be as much as thirty degrees), and then the children would racket about among the houses until their mothers called them in for their baths and put them to bed. Then they'd sit out on their doorsteps chatting to the neighbors. They'd make plans for tomorrow's laundry, darning, weeding, and watering the vegetable patch.

Jasna too lived like that for a month, until the people of Presjeka heard a roaring sound. Or rather a rumbling sound: monotonous, dull, muffled but clearly audible. It was coming along the valley from Nevesinje, more than twelve miles away. The valley, or rather the plain, is a broad corridor closed on both sides by the formidable Velež and Crvanj mountain ranges. It's like a flat table covered with sparse grass and stones. That is why, in spite of the distance, it was so easy to hear the noise.

It was the sound of grenades exploding. The people of Presjeka didn't know what was happening in the town until the first survivors arrived from there. "They're murdering us," they said.

The first killings of Muslims in Nevesinje took place on June 10, 1992. The first to be killed were the rich. Then it continued at random.

## Wolves

At four in the morning on June 22, Serbian grenades fell on Presjeka.

One woman was killed. (Who remembers her name today?)

Houses were set on fire. The heat intensified. People grabbed their clothing, food, and children.

In terror they headed for the Crvanj mountains.

They hid in the forest. They couldn't go any farther, into the great, bright, open space.

Night fell. They set off back across burned-down Presjeka to the village of Kljuna.

They met Muslims from Kljuna and other neighboring settlements. Among them there were also people from Mostar whom the Serbs had captured and for some unknown reason let go again.

In Kljuna they had to abandon seventeen old people who could not walk across the mountains: Jasna remembers a man parting from his mother because he couldn't carry her. He left her a little food. He had a wife and children—he had no choice.

The abandoned old people did not need the food they had for long.

Their throats were cut. Their dead bodies were torn apart by wolves that dragged their bones all over the district.

## The Cage

The children, women, and men all walked on, not knowing where. Among them were some foresters who worked in these forests and assured the others that they knew where they were going. They would lead them all to Mostar—that was what they promised. In Mostar it was already calmer; the Serbs had left the city because they had made a deal with the Croats. Earlier they had killed a hundred people and thrown their bodies on a rubbish tip. (That was how Jasna's two cousins had died.)

The children, men, and women walked up Mount Velež in rain and hail, on cold nights and blazing-hot days. It was hard going. Jasna had her little daughter in her arms, while Hasan carried their son.

Aila was nine months old.

Amar was four years old.

On the fourth day a grenade landed just beside the refugees. It must have fallen by accident, as there was sporadic fighting going on between the Serbs and the Croats in the area. There was a shout, panic, and a headlong rush. The explosion divided the refugees into two groups. Jasna, Hasan, his brother and his wife, and all the children ended up in the smaller group. Jasna's mother-in-law was in the larger one. The larger group had more luck. The foresters, who knew the local mountains, also disappeared along the way.

On they went, Jasna, her husband, their children, her husband's brother, his wife, and their children. For four days several dozen people went around in circles in the forest, as if trapped in a cage, hungry and thirsty.

On June 26, seven Serbian soldiers, armed to the teeth, came up behind them. The women held the children close, and the men threw their pistols into the bushes. The soldiers did not swear or insult them. "Don't be afraid," they kept repeating, and told the group to go to the Velež pasture.

There were some villages there, only they were Serbian now.

In one of the villages there was a school. Outside the school the Serbian men organized the selection efficiently:

women and children to one side of the road, Muslim men
to the other.

With as much contempt as they could muster, the Serbian
women shouted, "Whores! Bitches!"

The Muslim women bowed their heads.

But Jasna was watching the other side of the road. She
saw them take Hasan away. No one knows where.

They came back with him an hour later. Hasan glanced at
his wife and shook his head as if to say that no good would
come of the situation.

"What'll we do with these guys?" asked one of the
Serbs.

"Let's wait for the commandant to get here," replied
another.

According to Jasna they were talking about Zdravko
Kandić. He arrived a few hours later, at about five in the
afternoon. He gave an order—Jasna heard it.

"Onto the trucks and off to Breza!"

At the time she didn't know what Breza was. Now she
knows.

### Rubber Boots

We are in the forest. There are a lot of caves here,
holes in the ground. There's also Gajova Pit—a place
identified by a witness. There are no witnesses with us—
they're all too frightened. But Sanja Mulać and Jasna
have talked to a witness, who told them, "Take a look in
Gajova Pit."

In Gajova Pit, or to be more precise, above it, the workmen
cut away the bushes and with a few turns of their spades open
up a large hole in the ground. We cannot see how deep it is.

Anyway, no one makes any effort to look into it—everyone has moved out of the way, under a tree. There Dr. Klonowski is putting on white plastic overalls and winding a towline around her waist. There are no speleologists—we'll have to manage on our own. We attach several more ropes to her line and throw the other end of the tangle around the nearest thick tree trunk.

Dr. Klonowski puts on some latex gloves, grabs a torch, and descends into the pit. It is irregularly shaped. We cannot see the bottom, nor can we see Dr. Klonowski anymore. But now and then she pulls on the line for us to slacken it a bit, and it's clear she wants to go down even lower. She is out of sight for five, ten, twenty minutes.

"There's nothing there," she finally says, poking her head above ground again and shaking insects from her hair.

"What?!" exclaims Jasna, losing her cool. "What do you mean, there's nothing there?"

Jasna was hoping that she might finally find some red rubber boots today.

### The Cellar

Night fell. The women and children were ordered to get on some buses, which until recently had been used to take lumberjacks into the forest.

They set off. In the suburbs of Nevesinje they were told to get out and go down into a cellar in the town's boiler house.

The door was bolted.

The women laid the children on the concrete floor.

The children were crying. There was nothing to eat or

drink and no toilet. There wasn't enough air (just one tiny barred window).

At dawn, a Serbian boy peeped into the cellar through the window. He must have been about seven or eight. Jasna asked him for some water for the children. As the boy went off, she thought he'd come back. She wasn't wrong.

"Alija fucked your mothers!" he shouted as he opened a bottle of water and emptied it in full view of the thirsty children. At the time, the Muslim Alija Izetbegović was president of Bosnia. "Get him to give you water!"

Jasna asked her son to pee into a bottle cap. "She drank it as if it were juice," she says of her daughter.

A second day came, then a third. A toilet was no longer needed, because the children had nothing to urinate.

On the fourth night, at about eleven, someone started banging on the door, swearing. There were several of them. They didn't have a key—they just battered the door down.

There were five of them, two with stockings over their heads.

Jasna was holding Aila in her arms, and Amar was standing close to his mother.

It was dark, and the men shone torches in the women's faces. One beautiful girl was saved by her seven-day-old son. "She's just given birth," said the men. "She won't be any use."

The women understood what the men had come for. They began to scream.

The men had already taken three: Fadila and two beautiful sisters.

They also took Mersada, the mother of two children. And Jasna.

Jasna tried to break free, but they seized her by the hair and beat her.

"You won't come?" They took out knives. "Then we'll slash your child's throat right in front of you."

She went.

Thirty women and twenty children were left in the cellar, including Aila and Amar.

### Imitation

It is August. Jasna is waiting for us at the Big Ben café.

She has a mature face, fine dark eyes (subtly underlined with eyeliner), lipstick (sometimes she smiles briefly), neat red hair, a gold chain, a camisole, green army trousers with pockets on the legs, and beige shoes. She is beautiful and proud. That's how she wants to be: "That's what my husband loved about me."

We are traveling together toward Nevesinje in the Serb Republic.

Jasna, now in sunglasses, is sitting in the front seat. "I was born here, and I died here."

She opens the window and the wind ruffles her hair. "Life is just an imitation."

We pass through a small town: there are people walking about and drinking coffee at the cafés.

"In every one of them I see a murderer."

### The Motel by the Lake

The five most beautiful women were taken to Lake Boraćko (there was a motel there, some tourist cabins, and an old leisure center), where the White Eagles—a

Serb paramilitary organization—were stationed. There were also some Serb soldiers there from Banja Luka and Knin, in red berets. They were drinking.

One of them was Petar Divjaković, known as Divjak. According to Jasna, he was the cruelest of them all. Now he lives in Novy Sad (in Serbia) and has a happy family.

The women were split up. Jasna was taken to the motel. On the way she took off her gold rings and bracelets and hid them in her pockets, automatically, without thinking about it. They pushed her into a small room, no more than six square feet. Inside there was a man whose face Jasna no longer remembers.

She does remember the huge knife he had tucked into his belt.

He was sitting on a chair and told her to sit down opposite him.

"Where are you from? Are you married? How many children have you got?"

She answered.

"Is your husband a Muslim?"

She answered, and added that it was all the same to her if someone was Serbian or Muslim. You shouldn't judge people by their nationality or religion.

"*Balinka*! If it's all the same to you, why didn't you marry a Serb, so a Serb could fuck you?"

*Balinka* is a pejorative term for a Muslim woman in Bosnia, a way of insulting her.

Jasna lied, saying that she had had a Serbian boyfriend at school, but he hadn't wanted to get married.

"What was his name?" the man immediately asked.

The whole time he kept his piercing gaze on her. She

was afraid that the instant she looked away, he'd cut her throat.

She looked him straight in the eye.

"Goran," she said, giving the name of a boy from school who had sat on the front bench. And added his surname.

"When you get married, you get a lot of gold, don't you? Where's your gold?"

She thought that if she admitted she'd hidden it, he would kill her.

"It got left behind in Mostar."

"I'll just have a look in your pockets," said the man, lowering his voice and taking the knife out from under his belt. "God himself won't help you if I find something."

She thought that was the end.

She prayed to Allah that she might be shot, not killed with a knife.

The man stood up, came over to her, touched her, and went back to his chair.

"I believe you."

Some other men came in—three, four of them.

Among them was Petar Divjaković, the one who now lives in Novy Sad and has a happy family.

Then the rape began.

### Questions that Are Not Asked

"The rape began." That is all Jasna has to say about it. But she says it out loud. In Bosnia Jasna Ploskić may be the only woman to admit publicly that she was the victim of ethnic rape: the Serbs raped her because she is a Muslim.

Other rape victims keep quiet—they feel disgraced.

They even hide their disgrace from their husbands (if their husbands have survived).

But there are also some women here who will—discreetly—tell precisely how they were raped. International justice demands that they give an exact account. In these accounts they keep repeating certain details: several men, a dark room, a punch in the face, concrete, being undressed with a knife...

We're not going to ask Jasna any questions. We are not a tribunal.

### First Name and Surname

"In every one of them I see a murderer," repeats Jasna. "But when I'm at home, in Mostar, whenever I look at them, I think differently: they weren't all killers, were they? Every crime has its own first name and surname."

The crimes in Nevesinje included the murders of five hundred civilians.

Novica Gušić was commander of the Serbian army in Herzegovina. Not long ago Edina Kamenica, a journalist from the Sarajevo daily paper Oslobodjenje, called him in Belgrade, where he had fled. She asked him about those days in Nevesinje.

"Why don't you ask me about the mass graves of Serbs dating from 1941?" he replied.

People say that Zdravko Kandić—the one who ordered the men to be taken to Breza—is now living somewhere near Trebinje, but no one knows exactly where.

Until recently Krsto Savić, known as Kićo, the former police chief, was in prison in Foča (Serb Republic). He is suspected of murdering a Serb *vojvoda* (leader) after the war was over. We were in Foča and tried to talk to Kićo, because we wanted to ask him about that June in Nevesinje. But he wasn't in prison anymore. Through a decision of the Serbian court, even though there has been no verdict yet, he had been released and would remain at liberty pending trial. Where does he live? That we cannot know.

## Tidying Up

Jasna now knows what *breza* means. That is what they call the surrounding woods. On May 18, 1999, a mass grave was opened up here, a hole about two feet deep, with twenty-seven incomplete bodies (Dr. Klonowski took part in the exhumation). It was a secondary mass grave.

Jasna knows that toward the end of August or September 1993, on the orders of Zdravko Kandić and his superior Novica Gušić, four people went to a pit (a so-called primary grave) to transport some bodies. To Mount Velež, to another hole in the ground. They needed to tidy up, because the first United Nations forces were entering Nevesinje.

A few years later, Jasna spoke to one of the people who carried the bodies. Nowadays she regards him as a brother.

So there were two exhumations. Some of the bones were found in one pit, and some in another. Part of the frame of someone's glasses was found in one, a broken-off part in the other.

The first pit, the primary grave, was thirty feet deep. Above the pit, 144 cartridge cases and some telephone cables were found. (Were they tied up in advance?) No one knows if they were killed right after being brought from outside the school on June 26, 1992, or the next day. On most of their watches the date display stopped on June 28.

Jasna found her husband.

Dr. Klonowski stuck his skull back together.

There was a funeral.

## Trees

We travel down a flat, wide valley toward Presjeka. We drive through the village where Jasna's father was born, and where she was born too. This village has not been entirely destroyed—nowadays there are Serbs living in the Muslim houses.

Now we're in Presjeka. Where? On the right-hand side of the narrow tarmac, the place is barely visible. The gray stone skeletons of houses (with no roofs, windows, or doors) have blended in with the stony slopes of Mount Crvanj behind them. As ever, it's blazing hot, the air is still, and it's silent.

But there is some greenery, which tells us there was once a village here, some settlements. (We are familiar with similar villages in the south of Poland, in the Lemkowszczyzna area of the Carpathians.) There are pear trees, plums, walnuts, elder, and rowan; trees, saplings, bushes, and creepers are all pushing their way with impunity into hallways, cellars, bathrooms, sitting rooms, kitchens, larders, workshops, stables, cowsheds, classrooms, a café, and a shop. Nothing stops the onward march of the trees; there is no one to fell them or prune their branches. Copious rain in spring and autumn keep them alive.

Several of the houses are new; protruding here and there from behind the ruins, they don't fit in with the rest of the scene. They are covered with stucco and have windows and red roofs. Life is returning to Presjeka.

An elderly woman and man come out to greet us. They are happy to see Jasna. They are dressed as if they were expecting guests: he is in beige trousers with sharp creases and a blue shirt with a collar. She is in a light headscarf, a neat blouse, and a patterned skirt.

They don't have any children. No one ever visits them.

The Serbs don't come through here.

That day, when they were wandering about in the mountains and the grenade fell right beside the refugees, the couple ended up in the larger group. The group that was luckier.

They returned to Presjeka recently and, with the help of a European Union grant, they have rebuilt their little house. She has sown some flowers and planted some bulbs. Using rubber hoses, he has reconstructed part of the old water-supply system. They have running water and a nice bathroom.

No buses run to Presjeka.

Once a week a Serb comes from Nevesinje and sells them coffee, sugar, and flour. He has no work, so he thought up this business for himself.

They have a monthly pension of a hundred marks, which they use to buy essentials.

He has kidney disease and ought to have an operation, but there is nowhere to have one. Everywhere is too far away.

The couple rarely talk to the few neighbors who have recently returned. Their houses are scattered (each has rebuilt his own) and they'd have to walk for a long time. And the sun is burning hot. No one has the strength; they're all old and sick. In the evening it's dark and quiet, so you feel too frightened to go out among the ruins.

In winter there will be waist-high snow. They used to have firewood from their own forest. Now there's no forest (the Serbs cut it down), so they have to buy wood, transport it here, and chop it.

"There are no young people here," they say. "Life has returned to Presjeka but only temporarily. These are the village's final years."

There is a cemetery in Presjeka. The old upright gravestones (from Turkish times, and from Tito's era) are leaning over.

There are no new graves. For the past nine years no one has died here.

Both the man and the woman pray that Allah the Merciful will take them at the same time.

They don't ask Jasna any questions. They know what she went through.

### Good News

In the motel by Lake Boraćko the rape victims were herded into a makeshift prison. Jasna, Fadila, and Mersada were there, but the two beautiful sisters were missing.

There were twelve other prisoners. They said they were Croats from near Mostar.

The Serbs came at night (Chetniks, that's what Jasna calls them). They tortured the men.

The women covered their heads with blankets.

The torturers boasted to the women that they could even kill children.

At dawn a man came and took Jasna out of the prison. He told her that he liked her very much, that he wanted to sleep with her, and so on. She told him about her husband and children, and that she didn't know what was happening to them.

He took her to a tourist cabin, where the two beautiful sisters were waiting. They had already been through a lot.

They came from Presjeka, which is why Jasna is alive today. The older sister worked at a textile factory in Nevesinje and knew the local commanding officer, Radoslav Soldo.

He promised to save them.

Petar Divjaković promised to kill them.

Radoslav asked the women if they had a Serbian woman friend in Nevesinje who would give them shelter.

"Yes, we do," said the sisters. "We've got Sveta."

At Lake Boraćko there was one other decent man whom Jasna now mentions. He was a student from an Orthodox seminary who had been forced to join the army. He asked Jasna why she was crying.

She told him about the children in the cellar, with no food or water, and without their mother.

"For shame!" he cried. At this point Jasna would like to say his name, but she can't remember it.

At dawn Radoslav took her and the two sisters to Nevesinje. What happened to Fadila and Mersada, who were left behind with the tortured men? Jasna never saw them again, or those men either.

They are still missing.

The Serbian friend opened the door. "They'll burn my house down," she said, eyeing the women warily, and closed the door.

"Take me to my children," Jasna told Radoslav. (The two beautiful sisters did not have children.)

He told them to wait at a hotel. He assigned a soldier to protect them. "Have a coffee," he told them.

Meanwhile, he went to the Serbian police chief and the Serbian army commander. (We already know their names.) "I'll find out everything and come back for you," he said.

He came back an hour later and said something that Jasna will always remember: "I have good news. The children are well. Yesterday they were taken to be exchanged for prisoners from the Muslim side. Screw them—they gave us four corpses for a whole busload of living people."

There were supposed to be twenty children on the bus.

"Were my children there?" asked Jasna, leaping to her feet.

"Yes, they were."

Radoslav asked if they felt brave enough to cross Mount Velež on their own, to get to Mostar. The children should be there.

"And you'll find your husband there," he said.

"We'll go."

He took them to the foot of the mountain and gave them some bread and canned food.

"May God allow us to meet again one day as people who can look each other in the eye. Be careful."

He pointed out a route for them across Velež. He warned them that if they fell into the hands of the Šešeljovs—the Serbian paramilitaries—not even Allah could help them: "No one will save you. Or me."

He drove away.

They started crawling. They only stood up once darkness had fallen.

Until recently, no one but Muslims had lived on the

slopes of Mount Velež. Now there was only cattle in the pastures.

"Come here, Glavica!" they heard a man say. "Oh, why don't you just drop dead?!"

The women burst into tears. They were sure they were done for—the end had come.

The man was shouting at a cow.

"A Chetnik can't possibly know the name of a local cow," said one of the women.

"Wait!" they shouted.

The man, or rather boy, started to run away.

"We're on your side," they shouted after him.

"Allah himself sent me to meet you," he said once he had calmed down. "You're walking straight toward a village full of Šešeljovs."

The Šešeljovs are famous for their cruelty.

The women rested in the Muslim herdsman's tent.

Then they were shown the way to a Muslim village, where they met up with some Muslim soldiers.

At night they were transferred to Mostar, to the western district, where a refugee camp had been set up in a children's home.

Jasna felt such joy—she spotted her mother-in-law.

"Where are the children?" Jasna asked. "Where is Hasan? The children arrived here yesterday," she said, looking around her. "A whole busload."

"Jasna! No children have arrived. There aren't any children here."

## Two Women

On the other side of Mt. Crvanj (not far from Lake Boraćko) is Borisavac Pit.

For centuries the local people have said that it is bottomless.

But now (at the end of August) we know that it has a bottom: you only have to go seventy-five yards down a narrow chimney. Down there lie some bones; lamps are lit, and people are working.

At the mouth of the pit there is a crowd of people, including Jasna, standing next to Dr. Ewa Klonowski, who broke her leg in another mass grave a month ago and so cannot work down at the bottom. A monitor has been set up for her and a camera has been lowered into the pit, so we can see what is going on down there. The relatives of the missing people are also watching. Dr. Klonowski is running the exhumation by radio. Piotr Drukier, a young anthropologist from Wrocław, is working down at the bottom. With him is Amor Mašović, head of the Bosniak Commission on Missing Persons.

In Borisavac Pit we are expecting to find the bones of nineteen elderly people who were murdered in a nearby village in July 1992. From the account of a man who survived the execution it emerges that the bodies were thrown down here: into a bottomless pit.

Now the first white body bags are coming up. The workmen lay them out on the grass. The relatives of the missing people stand around as Dr. Klonowski examines the bones, identifying their age and sex.

The remains of two young women have been exhumed.

So these are different bones. Jasna was not expecting that.

"Could it be Fadila and Mersada?" she asks; her eyes are moist.

"It could," says Dr. Klonowski. "We'll have to check."

"And are there any children?"

"Piotr!" says Dr. Klonowski over the radio. "Have you got any children down there?"

"No, I haven't. Not so far."

### The Mothers' Luck

The children who went missing at Nevesinje in June 1992 were:

Baby Šipković (seven days old, no first name)
Asim Šipković (aged seventeen)
Huso Šipković (aged three)
Huso Aličić (aged eight)
Meho Aličić (aged seventeen)
Merima Aličić (aged five)
Nazika Aličić (aged eleven)
Saudin Aličić (aged five)
Salih Alibašić (aged sixteen)
Ajla Mahinić (aged one)
Ibrahim Mahinić (aged twelve)
Lejla Mahinić (aged seven)
Omer Mahinić (aged ten)
Amina Omerika (aged one)
Agan Ploskić (aged one)
Amar Ploskić (aged five)
Emin Ploskić (aged one)
Samra Ploskić (aged four)

Aila Ploskić (aged nine months)

"Today Aila would be ten years old," says Jasna, working out her children's ages. She has no photographs of her daughter. They hadn't had a chance to take any pictures.

Amar Ploskić, aged four, was wearing red rubber boots. He would have been thirteen now. In the picture Jasna shows us, he is sitting on a little bicycle.

Jasna is the only mother who survived the boiler house. The other mothers were luckier: they died along with their children. We don't ask Jasna about her children, such as what they weighed when they were born; how long she breastfed them; whether they were clever, jolly, and well behaved; or about the size of the red rubber boots.

*Today most of the people in Srebrenica have been
living there only since the end of the war.*

## Chapter 8

# *The Memorial*

The town of Srebrenica is in a green gully in the Serb Republic. There are houses, apartment blocks, a school, and an Orthodox church on the hill. It's hot. People are sitting outside houses that are not theirs. And they are staring. Someone is laughing. Crying. No one ever goes anywhere on foot. Or by car. Better not to.

But outside some of the houses we can see that something is going on. There's renovation under way.

Muslim women are reclaiming their old homes in the Serb Republic, renovating them using Serbian labor and then selling them to Serbs. Or trying to sell them. In neighboring Bratunac, the first few transactions have already been completed, but in Srebrenica there haven't been any.

The Serbs wanted a Serbian Srebrenica, but they don't want to buy the houses here. They say, "This isn't our home. This is a Muslim town, a town of death and bloodshed. And voices that come from God knows where. Whispers, screams, wailing." Apparently there are people here who sometimes hear the sound of five muezzins from five invisible minarets, calling the Muslim faithful to prayer, although they have been gone for years.

Today's inhabitants of Srebrenica can go to Sarajevo, Vogošća, Iljaš, Donji Vakuf, Bugojno, or Glamoč if they have the money for the bus. There they can go to the

Muslim authorities and cite the Dayton Accords to try to reclaim their houses. (It's the women who go and see the authorities—the men don't like to travel.)

Some Serbs are reclaiming their houses in the federation, then renovating them with European Union money. The Serbian women employ Muslim workmen there, then put the houses up for sale. That is what usually happens. For the money they get from the sale they buy houses in the Serb Republic, but not in Srebrenica. The authorities promised us they'd reopen the factories and the health spa here, the women say. They said there would be work. The health spa is still there, but no one wants to come here for a holiday. The authorities want to change the name of Srebrenica to Srbobran ("The Serb Defends"). They believe this will help to promote the city.

War will help, they say in Srebrenica. War might change something.

Not long ago in Potočari, under a tree in a field beside the road, the Muslim widows and mothers ceremonially unveiled a stone in memory of the massacre, inscribed "Srebrenica, July 1995."

And then, under police escort, they left the place they were driven out of several years ago.

There is some carpeting around the stone, but there is not even a pathway leading to it, just bare earth. No one is looking after it.

Now the Serb Republic authorities guard the Muslim monument to make sure no one damages it. A wooden sentry box, painted in the Serbian national colors, has been set up under the tree. A Serbian policeman has been put on guard. He sits on a chair with his feet propped on a tree stump. He has placed his hands on his knees and is sitting still, staring. He has to guard the Muslim stone. We ask him why he has to do that. He smokes a cigarette and throws away the butt.

*Greenhouses. Rizvanovići, 2001*

## Chapter 9

# *The Return*

That summer (1992), people stopped living in Rizvanovići, near Prijedor. Their living spaces, hallways, kitchens, and sitting rooms were taken over by rowan trees, acacias, and lilacs. The roofs began to cave in and the floors to rot. The dogs and cats disappeared. The doves flew away. Hazel bushes grew so vigorously on the roadside curbs that they met in the middle above the tarmac, creating a dense green tunnel.

The nights here can be black and foggy, and with no people around they must have been eerie.

Tonight it is quite pleasant. There's a full moon. People have put out their lights and are falling asleep.

### Gnashing

We are drinking coffee at Halima's house (she is forty-two).

"I have gotten used to it now," she says. "I have a wash and get into bed. When I feel cold, I reach for that red blanket. I fall asleep without any difficulty, straight off, worn out by the long day.

"Sometimes he visits me. I don't like those visits. What does he come for? I know he'll be gone very soon. I know that from the beginning. I turn over to face the wall.

"'Go away,' I say. 'Go back where you came from.' I'll wake up in a moment.

"He doesn't listen. He sits here, on the sofa bed, at the foot. He smiles. He doesn't even embrace me. If only he'd explain what happened. Where did he go that day?

"If only he'd ask about the child.

"I could talk and talk, without stopping. About how I cleared the bushes, for example. I ruined my hands that time, and my back.

"Nothing. He is silent, like a stone. He just stares, as if he knows everything. Sometimes I feel angry with him for leaving me like that.

"Just then our son might come in from the other room (at two or three in the morning?), take another blanket from the armchair and cover me with it.

"I get up with the sun.

"'Same thing again, Mama,' says my son. 'You were gnashing your teeth in the night again.'

"'Was I crunching again? Sorry.'

"'As if you were eating a stone.'

"I drink some coffee, open the window, and look out. The world is still there."

## The Last Day of the Holidays

The children are making noise, the women are hanging out the washing, and the men are sifting sand. The cement mixers are roaring, and houses are rising. There are bare brick walls all around: on the left-hand side of the road and on the right, next to the tarmac, in a field, or further on by the woods. There are almost thirty new houses. From the new windows—if they look west—there will be a view of Prijedor or—if they look east—a dense clump of bushes. The bushes are growing over the remains of the old houses, where no one lives anymore.

It will be lovely in Rizvanovići. But not yet this year.

Now the cement mixers are silent.

The men's holiday is coming to an end, and now they must go back where they came from. Their suntanned, pretty wives are packing their cases and a few bags of red peppers each. (Peppers bought in the German supermarket will never be as good as these, from the land of their fathers.) Colorfully dressed children are already sitting in silver Mercedes-Benzes, in child safety seats, waving goodbye to us. Each one has been given a bottle of mineral water for the journey.

There is no drinking water here. The water supply has not worked for years, and the few wells are covered over with sheet metal, fiberboard, or plywood. No one makes use of them, no one even looks into them.

Then come the final kisses and tears. The local housewives are standing in the road, seeing their relatives off.

They will miss their loved ones, especially the smallest children: nappies on the line, dummies falling to the floor.

The last time someone was born in Rizvanovići was nine years ago.

## Peppers

On the edge of the village there are some greenhouses. They were built with money from Austrian farmers and Italian pensioners. They are owned by the Bridges of Friendship Association, established by the local housewives. They work here and they are lucky, because in

Bosnia (and in the neighboring villages too) most of the women are unemployed.

The women used to work in Prijedor: in offices, libraries, shops, and factories. Now there is no work for them in the city. Even if there were, no inhabitant of Rizvanovići would go and work there. After all, in Bosnia work starts with sharing a cup of coffee.

What would a woman from here have to talk about with people from Prijedor over coffee?

About how their faces were painted black? They'd have to ask who those men were.

About the white towels? They'd have to ask what they were used for.

About the blown-up church? About the mosques? They'd have to ask who spared the Orthodox churches.

About the dances by the river? They'd have to ask why there's no one left to dance with anymore.

In the greenhouses they grow peppers. The peppers are sown in growing frames twice a year: toward the end of February and in August. They have to prepare the earth, which is done with the help of some American earthworms donated by someone from abroad. Whatever grows has to be planted out in March and September. It has to be weeded every day and watered each evening.

As they work the women talk about the shopping they used to do:

"Collar size forty-one."

"Height one meter eighty."

"Shoe size forty-three."

"Forty-five."

"There was always a problem with the big sizes."

They have to shut the greenhouses at night so the peppers won't freeze, and open them before dawn so they won't get scorched.

"We used to play volleyball on the beach." Now they're talking about their holidays in Croatia.

"The children used to make sand castles."

"One of them nearly drowned but my husband saved him. It looked really dangerous."

The harvests are in summer and winter, and in January the peppers are at their most expensive, especially the kind from Rizvanovići, grown without any chemical sprays. The women sell the peppers, as well as tomatoes, cucumbers, beans, asparagus, and potatoes, at the market in Prijedor, three miles away.

They don't like going to the city. They only do their business at the outdoor market: they sell their vegetables and then do their shopping there. It is the cheapest place for clothes, shoes, cosmetics. It's all rubbish, but no one here can afford the shops.

Today Jasminka (head of the association, aged thirty-something) bought a steel-gray bathing suit. She paid twenty marks for it and is happy with her purchase.

"Look! Look!" she says, winking at us.

Tomorrow she and her girlfriends are off to the River Sana.

They'll pack some *burek* (thin pastry baked with meat), *kefir*, and iced tea into their baskets. Although they have the Sana nearby (the river is especially lovely here), they're going to Sanski Most, twenty miles away. To their own folk, to the Bosniak-Croat Federation.

Rizvanovići (and the neighboring villages, Bišćani,

Rakovčani, and Hambarine) were always Muslim. But for several years they have been surrounded on all sides by purely Serbian settlements. And Serbian Prijedor (which before 1992 had a Muslim majority). Today they are entirely surrounded by the Serb Republic.

## A Fine Sight

In the evening, at Kemila's place (she's thirty-four):

"There are some Czech soldiers stationed not far away from us. As soon as we came back they were always coming by, so we'd feel more at ease. Now they keep an eye out and bring us water.

"They're tall, blond, and well built.

"They say, '*Ahoj!*' and tell us we're pretty. Maybe they say the same thing to the neighbors. The neighbors put on makeup and face powder. Me? I've already had my love life.

"Our teenage sons love the uniforms.

"They treat us to sweets. They're going to fix the electrical wiring for us.

"They like it when we make *japrak* for them. It's meat wrapped in vine leaves. It's a fine sight to see them eating it. They praise us, saying it's just like home.

"The commanding officer watches out to make sure they don't stay at our place too late. They are disciplined, as they must be in the army. We pack them some cake for the road.

"The neighbors may also be counting on them for something. But every six months the soldiers change over, they have to leave. They go home to their Czech girls.

"What normal person would stay here? Who would have children here? Why on earth?"

## The Beach

Unlike the other rivers here, the Sana isn't very dirty. There are no old gas cookers, washing machines, cables, television sets, bicycle frames, tractor tires, or wrecked cars floating in it. Sometimes there's a bottle or a can, nothing big, so you can bathe.

The Muslim women take off their trousers, blouses, and dresses.

They open bottles of oil and rub it onto each other's backs. They're laughing.

They go into the water and swim. Then they come out onto the riverbank and dry each other off.

There are some men on the beach.

The women lie down on a blanket. They have something to eat and drink, and talk about the peppers.

They return home in the evening. One of them gets on the tractor, while another primes a pump and pours water from a concrete basin into a metal tank standing on a trailer.

The tractor won't move, so they call in a Serbian mechanic from Prijedor.

The mechanic has just come from church; he is polite, climbs into the cab, asks questions about the peppers, and fixes the tractor.

The women water the peppers and close up the greenhouses for the night. They wash and go to bed.

## That July

At Fadila's house (she's thirty-one):

"It's nice here at our place, isn't it? The ground floor's finished, so we have somewhere to live. What is there to fear? What can they do to me? Kill me?

"I was born here, and I'm going to go on living here, whether the bastards from Prijedor like it or not.

"I used to travel through Prijedor to work. We used to like going to the cafés by the river there. In the evenings we used to go to concerts there; we used to dance and drink Coca-Cola.

"Those days will never return.

"I worked nearby, in Keraterm, in a ceramics factory. We used to make fire-resistant coils, heaters, vases, ashtrays, and figurines.

"Our people used to work in the mines, at Ljubija, Tomašica and Omarska.

"First of all they sacked us. Me and my husband, and all the Muslims. They cut off our electricity here and turned off the water. We sat in the cellars because they were shooting. The point was to make us feel afraid. And I was.

"There were a large number of Muslims living in the city. The Serbs took them away to camps. But at that point I don't think we knew about that yet. Who would have believed it?

"Finally they announced on the radio (we had a radio that ran on batteries) that we were to stay at home because they were going to register us.

"It was July 20, 1992, seven in the morning. In accordance with the instructions, we hung white flags in our windows.

"They came from all sides, they drove up in personnel carriers. They surrounded Rizvanovići and the neighboring villages. They were wearing various uniforms: black, navy blue, and camouflage. Serbs.

"The ones in navy blue came from Prijedor. They had

their faces smeared in black, dark glasses, knives, batons, rifles, and white towels on their shoulders.

"They went from house to house. I can still hear their voices now—friends from primary school, from technical college, from the cafés by the river. I would have gone to the International Criminal Tribunal at The Hague and told the international judges about them. But who there wants to listen to me? Who'd have the time?

"Some people managed to escape. My husband went too. He ran away to the forest.

"I never miss a single exhumation. He was tall, dressed in a sky-blue T-shirt and green work trousers. I'll recognize him; I'll be able to say goodbye. How long can you go on missing a man you know will never come home again?

"Those who stayed in the village were dragged out of their houses. They killed them in the backyards. Or over there at the crossroads, in the field, in the meadow. The teenagers too.

"They forbade the women and children to go near the windows. They shot at the panes.

"They wiped their knives on the white towels and went on their way.

"Now I dig up bones along with the potatoes. Is this my husband? Or my brother, who had just come back from Germany on holiday two days earlier? There are bones sticking up all over the place, floating in the wells.

"They dragged the woman next door up to the attic. They knew her from Prijedor; she worked for a Muslim in a restaurant. They raped her, killed her, and went on their way.

"Some people who were still alive were packed onto trucks.

They drove away into the unknown. Now we know they went to death camps, where they were tortured. Maybe my husband suffered there too. I would like to know how. What did they do with his body?

"I know that body by heart; I'll recognize it.

"That night, which I'd prefer not to remember, was exceptionally black. The Serbs shot out all the lamps. It was as silent as the grave. We women grabbed the children and raced to another house as fast as we could. More than one of us tripped over the corpse of her husband. We wanted to be together, in a group. A board creaked, a dog began to bark, but we were afraid to move. We wept so quietly we couldn't even hear each other.

"The sun came up. We went up to the windows. I need to forget what I saw.

"They smashed their way in to get the woman next door, two women.

"Here we have a mother who was raped by seven men. And her daughter, who was nine years old. And they killed her son. He was lying by the barn—she buried him with her bare hands. Do you want to talk to her?

"They took away money, jewelry, television sets, and cooking pots.

"They took tractors, machinery, and tools from the stables. Our village was rich—someone from each family had gone to the West to work.

"The next day came, then a third and a fourth. We sat inside hungry and dirty, with no water. The heat was unbearable. Flies were feeding on our husbands' bodies.

"They refused to let us leave the house to bury the dead.

"The corpses stank. It began to bother the men from Prijedor too. They found a neighbor who was eighty years old. They ordered him to collect the bodies from the road, from the meadows. He shifted them onto a truck by himself. He threw his own sons onto the pile last of all. He had two of them, and he threw them both onto it. Then they ordered him to sit on his sons, and drove away. Where to?"

### The Small Tractor

For their work in the greenhouses the women also need a rototiller, a bean planter, and a small, lightweight tractor that can be driven indoors. The small tractor is essential. One of the Serbs here has one, so sometimes they call him. And there's always some sort of problem.

A small tractor costs eight thousand Deutschmarks (about six thousand U.S. dollars).

They also need hoes, spades, rakes, forks, trolleys, and wheelbarrows.

The women want to have more greenhouses so more of them can work. For now there is enough work for forty-three. Each woman receives 150 marks (111 dollars) per month (plus a pension left by her late husband, making nearly 300 marks [222 dollars] in all).

Those who have not found employment (by far the majority) have a monthly pension of not much more than a hundred marks (seventy-four dollars). Or nothing, if their husbands were too young and worked for too short a time. They eat whatever they manage to grow: corn, potatoes, and eggplants.

That summer the women were eventually ordered

out of their houses. They were told to go to an area fenced off with wire. There they and their children were kept waiting for hours and hours in the sun, until some buses drove up and they were told to get in. They were beaten. They ended up in the camps at Trnopolje or Keraterm (in a ceramics factory), where they were told to get out. As they sat there with nothing to eat or drink, new women kept being brought in from all over. The place soon became crowded. Then they were told to get back on the buses and were beaten again.

They were driven to the front and told to keep walking across the lines to their own people.

First they went to live in refugee centers; later they occupied some empty houses that belonged to Serbs who had escaped to their own side. Some of the women went abroad, mainly to Germany. When the peace treaty was signed in 1995, the Bosniak women were asked to leave Germany, so they went back to their own country.

And, in accordance with the treaty signed at Dayton, the Serbs have been going back to their old homes too. That may be how it looks on paper, but nothing has changed since the war: they usually come back to vacate and to sell their houses. The authorities empty the houses of their illegal tenants (they evict them) and hand the property back to the owners.

The Muslim women decided to go back to Rizvanovići, now in the Serb Republic. At first they didn't recognize the village—the farmyards were covered in a jungle of vegetation. They cleared away the bushes. Some had got into the walls of the houses, which were no longer fit for anything.

They set up home together in a ruined office building or in tents.

Then they tried to get grants from the European Union. The EU is happy to give money to those who go back to their own area. In this way, Europe aims to erase the effects of the ethnic cleansing that was committed here.

The women were given some money for building materials. They had to buy them and start the building work within forty-five days. Anyone who failed to get started in that time had to give back the money.

They had no money to pay workmen, so they called their relatives in Germany, France, Sweden, and Austria—every place where inhabitants of Yugoslavia had gone to live in the past—and asked the men to come and help them. Anyone who could come did so, on holiday with their wives and children.

Anyone who couldn't come sent money. The women also went to Prijedor and looked for workmen there.

As there is no work in the city, the Serb bricklayers have been willing to build houses for the Muslim women.

### The Old Woman

In the garage where Mersada lives (she is seventy-four):

"Whoever did this, I hope one day feels what I am feeling.

"You see other people's children and grandchildren and you cry.

"I had no daughters, just two sons. I have no husband, no one.

"They have now found one of my sons for me.

"My daughter-in-law came from Sweden for his funeral. She said she was getting married again. My granddaughter will have a new father. And that's as it should be.

"I wake at four in the morning. I don't get up—why should I?

"Though, when they put freshly dug-up bones on display at Sanski Most I go there.

"Your own children always want to help you. Other people's children don't even look in. They won't ask whether you've got enough to eat.

"People changed after the war. They don't visit each other; they don't laugh.

"Lonely old women don't get grants. Europe doesn't want to rebuild our houses. We don't contribute to development.

"My cottage is gradually being rebuilt—a woman from abroad helped me. One day she came to visit me, and saw that I was living in a garage.

"Everyone in Bosnia knows Dr. Ewa. She digs up bones here and identifies people. She found my son for me and has promised to find the other one."

## The Well

In the first few days of September there is a commotion in Rizvanovići. There's going to be an exhumation (not the first one here and certainly not the last). Dr. Ewa Klonowski, the anthropologist, will conduct the exhumation.

There are three bodies in the well: two men and one woman. Who are they?

Probably no one from around here. It might be a Catholic

priest from Prijedor and his old parents. Croats. Witnesses say the Serbs brought them here from the city three years after that summer, in 1995. They were led toward a large clump of trees in the suburbs (in other words, in Rizvanovići). The priest was never seen again. Now we can see the bones.

The women have come to take a look. But some of the mothers are thinking about something else. Until now their children have been taught at Muslim schools in Sanski Most or Lušci Palanka. Recently the monthly bus tickets have gone up in price, and the mothers haven't enough money for the daily journey. In the last few days, it has become possible for the children from Rizvanovići to go to Serbian schools in Prijedor. They will have their lessons in Cyrillic. How will the Serbian teachers treat them? And what about their Serbian contemporaries? Will they talk to each other? About what?

In Rizvanovići the exhumation is over, and the team is moving on to the village of Ljubija, where a mass grave has been found in an open-cast mine. It's a big hole, 250 feet deep, a month's work, 372 bodies. Some of them have identity cards on them.

They are the men from Rizvanovići.

*"Bones speak to me," says Ewa Klonowski, Lušci Palanka, 2000*

## Chapter 10

# Ewa at Mejra's House

Who would have expected it—joy in Mother Mejra's house. People have come from all over to keep her company today. There's great relief; it's the end of the road and she can finally sleep peacefully. There's going to be a funeral, prayers, and a grave. Two graves. Mejra won't let anyone cry: "We'll show Nebojša—we must be dignified."

We wanted to go and see Nebojša B. with Dr. Klonowski. He lives nearby. But Mejra won't let us do that either: "You needn't go, it's not the right time yet."

Nebojša B., the man who used to be the boyfriend of Mejra's daughter, Edna, is now a policeman in Prijedor.

When the war broke out, Nebojša became an interrogator at Omarska, where Edna was a prisoner. He tortured and raped her.

Edna's brother, Edvin, was also seen at Omarska. He was tortured in front of his sister.

Edna Dautović was born on March 18, 1969. She was an education student.

Edvin Dautović was born on August 13, 1965. He was an electrician.

Now the imam (young and handsome, wearing an expensive pair of spectacles) is getting ready to recite the Yasin Sura for the dead, as the Koran commands. In the kitchen the women are making roast lamb and baklava. Mejra takes a small tablecloth from the cupboard and throws it energetically over Ewa's knees. "Legs! Cover your legs!"

Tactless Dr. Ewa! Not only did she sit with the men (the women are in the next room), she also dressed in too short a skirt. She doesn't have a scarf on her head, and on top of that she keeps chatting. And the imam is staring at her.

Dr. Klonowski has already dug up two thousand bodies in Bosnia. She has fished them out of wells, hauled them out of caves, dug them out of rubbish tips or from under piles of pig bones.

Thanks to Ewa we are now sitting at Mejra's house, listening to the imam reciting the words of the Yasin Sura: "Surely We give life to the dead, and We write down what they have sent before and their footprints, and We have recorded everything in a clear writing."

### The Book

It was the spring of 1992, the beginning of the war. The Muslims from Prijedor—where Mejra lived with her husband and children—were taken from their houses (from the street, from work, from the shops) to camps in Omarska, Trnopolje, or Keraterm. Or straight into the forest.

The recently published *Book of Missing Persons from the Prijedor District* contains more than three thousand names in alphabetical order. Most of them are men's names. The book is fat and heavy. Only nine photographs fit on each page. On page 88 Edna and Edvin look out of their pictures, next to the names of some men called Ismet, Derviš, Sead, Esef, and Fikret, who don't have photographs. Their relatives must have fled from their homes in panic and didn't take any pictures with them. Afterward there was nothing left to go back for. Today Prijedor is in the Serb Republic, and there are Serbs living in the Muslims' houses there.

So the editors of the book had problems. Whenever they lacked a photograph, above the name of the missing person they put a fleur-de-lis—the emblem of Bosnia.

Many of today's eight- and ten-year-olds do not know what their fathers and older brothers looked like. They are too young to remember them. When they grow up, they are sure to start missing those faces. A fleur-de-lis in the book of missing persons will not be enough. They will want to see what his nose was like, what his cheeks were like, his beard and his hair, and the expression in his eyes. They will want to decide if they are at all like him. They will search through the archives at schools, offices, the army, and other workplaces. They will ask at newspaper, radio, and television offices. They will talk about their greatest wish: "I'd love to know what my father looked like. Maybe someone has a picture of themselves with him: at school, in the army, or on holiday together near Dubrovnik. Maybe someone will call…"

Maybe someone has a photograph of Ibrahim Ademović (born 1961), Esad Ahmetović (1968), Mirsad Cehić (1973), Azmir Celić (1971), Ajdin Dženanović (1983), Elvir Kararić (1976), or Elvir Selomović (1975). Maybe someone knows where they are. Their families want to have a grave.

"Maybe someone knows where they are." That's what Mother Mejra was asking about her children in the spring.

## A Jigsaw Puzzle

On July 24, 1992, a bus with a sign saying "student

transport" drove away after eleven at night to an unknown destination. On the bus were fifty passengers, some of whose names are known. Among them were two women: Sadeta (petite, over forty) and Edna (young and terrified). Her friends from the barracks helped Edna to get on, because she herself hadn't the strength. They envied her because she was going to be exchanged for prisoners from the Muslim side—she was going to her salvation. That is what they were told.

It was the third bus to leave Omarska that day. The people from the first two were found in Hrastova Glavica, lying one on top of another, 124 bodies in all, just men.

Dr. Klonowski exhumed them in December 1998. It was exceptionally cold (zero degrees Fahrenheit, sometimes worse), but at the bottom of the cave it was warmer (forty-five degrees). It took more than a week's work from morning to night. Counting up the victims was no easy matter, because of the time that had passed (it was six years since the massacre) and because of the cave's sloping bottom (six by eight yards). Once the muscles and cartilage of the dead had ceased to exist, the bones slipped down and got jumbled together.

Out of this assortment of skeletons, Dr. Klonowski puts people back together—probably no one in Bosnia is as good at it as she is. She gets up at dawn, eats on the run, and is ready for work before eight. She works until evening, without a break, without stopping for dinner. She does suspend further exhumations to give her time to assemble the skeletons she has dug up already, though.

Usually she starts with the pelvic bones, or sometimes (as at Hrastova Glavica) the foot bones because the rest are missing. She has knowledge, experience, and patience. She never gives up. She examines a hundred other exhumed bodies and matches bone to bone. Sometimes nothing fits; hours and days can go by. She complains, grumbles even; her back is killing her, her eyes ache, but she goes on searching. There can be no doubts: "It must be a perfect match," she says, as usual mixing English, Bosnian, and Polish. At last she finds perfectly matching ankle, tibia, fibula, thigh, and pelvic bones. Then the vertebrae: lumbar, thoracic, and cervical, followed by the skull, which is sometimes in pieces, in which case she sticks it back together. Finally the arm, elbow, and radial bones, then the wrist and finger bones. The jigsaw is finished, and there's a complete person.

Dr. Klonowski does not believe that God exists. She knows that the families for whom she is doing this do believe in God. There will be a Judgment Day and a Resurrection. "I would prefer them to stand before their Allah on their own legs, not someone else's," she says, "and for them to have their own skulls on their necks. For them to look all right when they rise from the dead."

### Fractures

Where did the third bus go from Omarska? In the spring that was something we didn't know.

In the spring, Dr. Klonowski conducted the identification of seventy-three bodies at the village of Lušci Palanka that she had exhumed from another mass grave, at Kevljani. She laid out the clothes in the village cultural center, on the terracotta floor in the auditorium. Earlier she had taken them off the bones and laundered them to restore their colors. If any hair was preserved, she washed that too.

The families of missing persons were then summoned via announcements in the newspapers and on the radio.

Whenever someone recognized some clothing, Dr. Klonowski would show them the teeth, then the complete skeleton (if it was complete). And she would ask questions such as: "Did your father limp?" "Did your brother sit or squat?" "Did your son have a hip operation?" and so on. Once this stage of the identification had been successful, she would take blood samples from the nearest relatives for a DNA test. A match between the DNA in the blood and the DNA taken from the bones establishes a family relationship beyond any doubt.

Among the families who came for the identification was a lovely gray-haired lady.

"I am Mother Mejra," she introduced herself. "I come here every Thursday. I help Dr. Ewa, and I comfort the families."

"This is Edvin," she said at the time, showing us some scraps of clothing. "My son. The sex matches, and the age, and the height, and the teeth. But Dr. Ewa isn't completely sure. They haven't done our DNA tests yet. I had Edvin"—she leaned over to adjust a trouser leg—"and I had Edna too. I know all about what happened to my Edna. Who beat her up, who raped her. It was Nebojša, her boyfriend from before the war. The only thing I don't know is where that bus went. Her clothes are nowhere to be found, not even a shoe, nothing."

Skeleton *KV* 014: multiple fractures of the ribs, mainly from the front and sides, but also from the back. Broken breastbone. Two vertebrae broken in the upper part of the torso. Broken right shoulder blade. Some of the fractures are new, inflicted a day, at most two, before death. The rest were healing—from a few days or weeks earlier. Is it Edvin?

When she learned all of these details, Mother Mejra changed her mind: this was not her son.

"I couldn't believe it," she says now.

So she didn't sign the documents. According to the procedure, if the closest relatives provide a signature, there is a costly DNA test.

The unidentified bodies (of the seventy-three, ten were identified) have been buried at Kozarac, near Prijedor, in the Serb Republic, as decided by the cantonal court. Earlier, Dr. Klonowski cut a fragment of bone from each skeleton just in case a DNA test would prove to be necessary later.

She took blood from Mejra and her husband, Uzeir. Despite the lack of the necessary signature, their samples were sent to a laboratory in Madrid, and a fragment of bone from skeleton *KV* 014 was sent with them.

Meanwhile, Ewa turned to something else—the next exhumation, in the nearby village of Donji Dubovik.

### The Pit

In May of this year the Hague tribunal asked the Bosniak Commission on Missing Persons to exhume the Lisac Pit, near the village of Donji Dubovik in the Serb Republic, in northwest Bosnia. There were supposed to be some bodies in this pit—or so a witness had informed the tribunal.

The names of the witnesses are kept secret. Usually it is a Serb—for their information they get some money, but how much is not known. They say that they saw (no one ever says they took part) how and where people were murdered, transported, and thrown into holes in the ground.

The witnesses identify the sites but do not take part in the exhumations. They are afraid to. Too many people come to the site: anthropologists (including Dr. Klonowski), forensic scientists, and medical technicians; police inspectors, police technicians, prosecutors, and judges; investigators from the Hague tribunal; representatives of the Bosniak Commission on Missing Persons, and representatives of the Serbian Commission on Missing Persons (there are sometimes murderers among them, a fact everyone knows); volunteers from American nongovernmental organizations (who are not clued into what happened here), interpreters, speleologists (when there aren't any, Ewa goes down into the pit to reconnoiter herself), electricians, digger operators, and workmen to do the worst jobs. There are also sappers, because the pits might be mined. They do not always arrive in time, but even then Ewa goes down to the bottom. There are also soldiers from the international forces (SFOR) who protect the convoy and lend Ewa ropes when the one from her car is too short. Ewa works at the bottom, assisted by a pathologist and a few workmen, while everyone else stays at the top. They lie in the shade and wait for the end of the day.

Not far from the village of Donji Dubovik the witness has placed a cigarette packet out in the fields in the spot where they have to dig. There are depressions and holes around it.

In the first few days of June (it was blazing hot!) the convoy set out for the exhumation. They found the cigarette packet in the fields, and the digger got moving. All the bushes around the site were cut down (which was the end of any available shade), and the four nearest holes were investigated. Probes were sent down. Nothing. The team went away.

The investigator from the tribunal spoke to the witness again. The witness promised to put out another cigarette packet. Apparently he did it at night. The convoy went out again and found the new cigarette packet, but it was in the same spot as before.

Someone from the team, an Irishman, went for a walk out of boredom. A short way off he came upon a pit covered by a huge stone.

A speleologist went down on a rope and came back up. He said the pit was sixty-five feet deep, a beautiful chimney-shaped cave: it had honey-beige walls and was full of stalagmites. At the bottom there were some clothes, blankets, and bones. He brought up a single skull as proof that they were human. There were a lot of skeletons, and Ewa later had trouble fitting the skull to the right bones.

Rope ladders were let down, replaced two days later by metal ones—better, because they're stiff. "Luxury," says Ewa. (One time her husband was sitting in an armchair at home in Iceland, watching television, and saw his wife on CNN going down into a cave with her back to the ladder. He called her with a stern reprimand.)

Now she has gone down into the Lisac Pit, facing the ladder. The pathologist has gone with her. It hasn't been possible to rig up a wooden platform—someone forgot to bring the pegs needed to fix it in place. So they have been standing on the bones (not good—Ewa is renowned within the team for her respect for each little bone). The bottom is sixteen and a half by five feet—too wide to brace your feet against the walls.

The electricians have lit up the cave: "It really is fabulous," says Ewa. That's not true—there's water dripping in her face; it's cold and slippery. There are rats running about, spiders, and other insects.

She has divided the bottom into sectors: *A, B, C, D, E,* and *F.* She has already roughed things out.

The bodies are piled on top of each other, incomplete, bent and twisted, or rolled up like pretzels. They have flown sixty-five feet down, hitting the walls of the chimney (as well as the stalagmites and stalactites). The bottom is even worse than at Hrastova Glavica. It is sloped, too, but in both directions. It's cone-shaped. "The skulls are like balls," says Ewa. "They've rolled against the walls."

The pit was like a box that someone had shaken. Everything inside it had been scattered. There were some blankets lying on top.

The execution was most certainly carried out in the nearby village of Donji Dubovik (the witnesses say it happened next to the Orthodox church). The victims were probably loaded onto carts, as no other vehicle could have gotten here. Right by the cave not even a cart would be able to manage, so the bodies must have been carried to the pit on blankets. The same blankets were used over and over again, and then thrown into the pit along with the final corpses.

The exhumation team has fixed up a system of ropes to bring out the bodies.

On the first day Ewa extracted nine bodies from what she was standing on. All men—Ewa can identify the sex at once. She packed each one into a plastic body bag and sent them up.

At the top Mother Mejra is waiting. Although she lives far away (three hours' drive), she has brought dinner for Ewa, roast meat and salad. The others have been helping themselves too.

Finally a platform has been suspended just above the bones, so Ewa has been able to kneel on the boards as she works.

On the second day sixteen bodies are extracted. Number 025 has a woman's pelvic bone. A skirt, tights, and a red sweater—an unusual one, because it buttons on the shoulder. And a string of pearls. Immediately the people who might be able to provide identifications have been brought down here.

"That's Sadeta," said the former female prisoners from Omarska. "That's how she was dressed when she got on the bus."

Sadeta Medunjanin, mother of Enes and Haris, a history teacher.

The former prisoners burst into tears.

Ewa has not told Mejra anything about the fact she probably already knows.

On Sunday (when the team was not at work), she and the young pathologist laundered the exhumed clothes in a baby bath.

Some more female remains were found on Monday (June 26), in Sector *E*, skeleton number 042, near the bottom. It's a woman, one of the first to be thrown in. She was much younger than Sadeta, as Ewa confirmed at once. Ewa packed her into a body bag.

Mejra was not waiting at the top. That morning she felt unwell and had been rushed to hospital. She did manage to give her husband instructions to go and take Ewa her dinner. "As I ate it," says Ewa, "I looked at Uzeir. If it had been Mejra, I might even have told her…"

Uzeir was once the head of a family and owner of a construction company. Now he is a shrunken old man (he was born in 1939). He has already had two strokes. He remains silent for days on end, and when he does speak he trembles from head to toe: he is being kicked by an invisible torturer, or else he becomes the torturer and torments an invisible victim. He doesn't like company.

"I didn't have the strength to tell him," says Ewa, "that the bus is there, that Edna is there."

## The Toy

Like the other passengers, Edna was first shot in the pelvis—just in case; earlier there had been cases of people running away under fire. Then she was shot in the chest.

That much Ewa was able to read from the bones. She talks about it dispassionately: "You have emotions, you don't sleep at night. I sleep badly here anyway. I wake up at three in the morning and see skulls with holes in them. They shot a guy—one, a second, a fiftieth. I can see that. But how is it possible for fifty men at a time to go meekly to their death? Why didn't they do anything? Why didn't they save themselves? A few murderers tell them to get off a bus. They meekly do it. They meekly stand against a wall."

She'd prefer not to ask herself any questions. "That destroys me, it demoralizes me. My job is to assemble bones. That way I can help. I'm not made for war."

At the Commission on Missing Persons they remember how Dr. Klonowski conducted an exhumation near Prijedor.

"I was digging with the knowledge that I'd found some children," she says. "It's all the same to me whether I dig up a child or an old person. Bones are bones. With the one difference that children have more small bones; they are less durable. And I came upon some small bones of the kind I was expecting to find. And a toy next to them—a Superman doll. I had to put it in a plastic bag. I couldn't do it. I was holding it in my hand, and the child's father was there above me. I felt as if I could no longer cope. I was about to start crying. I rationalized it to myself by thinking, 'Ewa, someone has to work here. Bones are bones. This is a toy found next to some bones. You must put it in the plastic bag and get on with the next body.'"

### The Hall

There are moments that bring Dr. Klonowski joy—the news from Madrid, for example: the DNA from skeleton *KV* 014 is from the son of Mejra and Uzeir Dautović.

And the next bit of news: the DNA from skeleton number 042 (Lisac Pit) is from the daughter of Mejra and Uzeir Dautović.

This is the point of Ewa's work, the point of her life's mission, claims her husband, who comes here on holiday in the summer. On these occasions Ewa takes him to work with her: "vacations spent on exhumations," she says. Her mission is endless: there are still at least ten thousand people waiting to be found and exhumed. Well over ten thousand need to be identified. In the places where Ewa doesn't go, no one is particularly concerned whether a skull fits a spine.

If five assorted bodies are dug up, at most they have to be divided into five bags and buried in five coffins.

If they were to assemble all the bones they dig up as painstakingly as Ewa does, there would be enough work for several anthropologists for a hundred years.

Although the other specialists here are quicker and less precise, even so the exhumations are going slowly. The work is financed by the International Commission on Missing Persons (established in the USA specifically for the former Yugoslavia). It is in no one's interests in Bosnia to do the exhumations quickly. "God forbid," says Ewa. "It'd be the end of the high incomes, careers, and trips to international conferences. The digging has to be done very gradually. It has got to last for years, until retirement. What about the mothers and widows? Who cares? Who's bothered about them? Nobody cares that I care. It grieves me, even though it's not my country and they're not my people. So I'm a complete idiot. But perhaps even people like them have a right to live, don't they?"

This autumn Ewa is mostly working in the suburbs of Sanski Most (for weeks she has been living in a hotel, and her apartment in Sarajevo has been empty). There, in a desolate spot, is a large hall. It used to be a warehouse for building materials, but now it stores human bones, and whatever has been found with them.

The hall is airy, so there are no smells. There are two hundred plastic body bags lying on the ground, including the ones from Lisac Pit. Along with the bones there are clothes, lighters, wallets, name-day photos, and elastic bands.

Visitors come—from the local area, from Sarajevo, Zagreb, Vienna, Hamburg, and New York—and take a look. They stop for a while over one of the bodies, move on again, talk to Dr. Klonowski (sometimes she holds them by the arm), nod their heads, pray, weep, and occasionally faint, in which case Ewa calls an ambulance.

Sometimes a journalist from Sarajevo drops in and asks Ewa why she is doing this.

"I don't know," she says with a smile. "There's something driving me. A need to do something good. As if I wanted, me alone, to right the wrongs caused by others. I have a rare profession, one that is needed here right now. I have to be here."

Not long ago, at a meeting of members of the American Academy of Forensic Sciences, a French friend asked Ewa the same thing.

"I do it because I'm crazy," she whispered in his ear.

He looked at her and in total seriousness replied, "I thought so."

Back at the hall—whatever happens in here happens quietly, in whispers. Ewa too speaks quietly when she is asked about her motivation: "I'm not trying to build a career—I'm too old for that. They are paying me now, but there were months in Sarajevo when I had to count my change to buy a roll because they hadn't given me a grant. I worked for free, and I can still work like that."

Mother Mejra comes into the hall. She knows this place inside out. Many a time she has taken a mother's arm and helped her to inspect body after body. Now she has come to see her daughter (she knows the good news from Madrid). On arriving, she hugs Ewa. Then she takes Edna's skull in her hands. "How good it is to know," she says. "What about Edvin? Can he be dug up? I must bury him beside Edna, together."

"Write to the chief of police," Ewa advises.

Since May, Edvin had been lying in Kozarac, in the Serb Republic, unidentified among the other unidentified bodies (seventh row, *KV* 014). The formalities had taken two months. Finally, once all the papers were ready, Mother Mejra organized an estate car and went to Kozarac. There she was joined by the Serbian police and some Serbian officials. Mejra found some workmen—Serbs as well—on a building site. She transported Edvin to the hall in Sanski Most and handed him into Ewa's care. Then she set a date for the funeral: Saturday, October 6, 2000.

Now we are standing outside the hall in Sanski Most (it is two hundred yards long and thirty wide). It's a cold autumn morning, and there's a mist. Mejra is pouring hot coffee from a thermos, offering it to the assembled throng, and greeting her less immediate relatives. "You're not to cry," she reminds a young woman. "We'll show Nebojša."

Mejra believes that Nebojša will stand before the Hague tribunal to answer for what he did in Omarska over eight years ago. In Mejra's view, God has already punished him for Edna. "He has a wife," she says, "but no offspring. That is the worst punishment of all."

Ewa is deep inside the hall. She greeted Mejra an hour ago and then went to work. She rarely has a moment to herself (for a rest, a walk, a coffee at a café, or a trip to the seaside). We can see her clearly: she is standing amid the white bags neatly laid out on the floor. She is holding a bone and wondering to whom it might belong. Someone calls her to the second row, fifth body on the right. She goes over—she is always at the disposal of the families. It is

Enes who wants to talk to her, the son of Sadeta, who was murdered along with Edna.

### Sadeta's Son

"They weren't pearls," says Enes about the necklace found with his mother's bones. "They were white stones from Lake Ohrid or, rather, gray ones. Mama got them from my father. She never wore gold; she didn't like it."

Sadeta Medunjanin, a history teacher from Prijedor, is now lying in the second row on the left-hand side. Her son will be organizing a funeral soon. Before that he would like to find his younger brother, Haris. He is expecting to find him here. Eight years ago he and his brother walked through the forest with some other people, in an attempt to make their way from Prijedor into Croatia. But they were unsuccessful: they fell into an ambush and were fired at. They ran headlong, as fast as they could, through the woods. Most of them survived, but Haris did not.

Haris Medunjanin was born in 1970. He was left somewhere in the bushes. Recently, Dr. Klonowski pushed her way through those thickets, gathering up bones. They were brought here, to the hall.

Perhaps Haris is already here, waiting for his brother to identify him.

So Haris was killed first, shot as they were on their way through the forest to Croatia. Enes got as far as Omarska, with his mother and father.

His parents were educated people, so at Omarska they were placed in the so-called first category. Enes was too, because he was a student.

The first category included the Muslim intelligentsia,

rich people, and those who had taken part in action against Serbian troops (thus it also included Edna and Edvin Dautović, Mejra's children).

The guards had a list.

Those in the first category were to be killed first of all.

First the prisoners were beaten. The guards and investigating officers beat them, but so did ordinary people from the area. Anyone could come inside the campgrounds as long as he was a Serb. He could pick up a heavy object (a bar, something made of metal, or a spade), choose himself a Muslim prisoner, and beat him.

Ordinary people from the local area (farmers? craftsmen? workmen?) took advantage of this opportunity and then went home.

Enes's father had just about every bone in his body broken. He died in his son's arms on the fifth day of their imprisonment. His bones have never been found.

That evening, before the bus left Omarska with Edna and Sadeta on it, Enes went to find one of his relatives to get himself a cigarette. Just then a guard whom they called Cigo came to Enes's barracks and read out the name Medunjanin. They had already nearly filled an entire bus for an exchange of prisoners (including Edna and Sadeta), but they still had four empty seats. So they were calling Enes. One of the prisoners ran to fetch him.

Enes decided to stay a little longer and finish his cigarette with his relative.

The guards cannot have had time to look for him. For some unknown reason they were in a hurry. The driver was already warming up the engine, so they called the next name on the list.

Enes would like to know who it was. Who went instead of him?

A few days later the guards read out another list. Their papers were in a mess; they weren't sure whom they had already taken away and who was left.

So once again they called out, "Enes Medunjanin!"

"Here," he replied.

"You're still alive?" said the guard, failing to hide his amazement.

The prisoners realized that they weren't taking people to be exchanged but to their deaths.

Enes realized what had happened to his mother. And that no one else in his family was still alive.

It was August 6, 1992. Once the foreign journalists had discovered it, the camp at Omarska was closed down. Pictures of the living skeletons behind the barbed wire went around the world.

The skeletons were ordered to get on a bus.

Enes sat somewhere at the back.

They set off.

They parked outside another camp, at Manjača.

The guards did not tell them to get out. They were drinking.

First they called a man called Krak, then someone called Ded, both from the first category. Right next to the bus they cut their throats—everyone saw it through the windows.

Then they called, "Medunjanin!"

He didn't reply.

So they took the men in turn, while getting drunker and drunker. They managed to kill seventeen men before their strength ran out.

Dawn broke. Those left alive were chased out into a parade ground and put in groups of six with the other prisoners. Some other guards arrived, the next shift at the camp at Manjača. They herded the men into a stable next to the camp and told them to get undressed. They were counting on finding some valuables or money in their clothes (or, rather, their rags). Enes saw the guards from Omarska coming toward him. He spotted a gate and hid behind it. Then someone closed the gate.

"I think Allah himself must have done it," he says now.

It was the main gate of the camp. The guards from Omarska saw Enes running in there and tried to go after him, but they were not allowed in, because the local commandant insisted on observing the international conventions that said no one from the outside who is armed has the right to enter a prisoner-of-war camp.

It was a concentration camp, not a prisoner-of-war camp.

Enes hid in one of the barracks, only came out for meals and quickly went back inside. He was there for almost a month, until once again he heard: "Medunjanin!"

This time they were referring to his father. The Muslim side had given his name—they wanted him (and several dozen others) in exchange for some Serbian prisoners of war.

"Your father's not here, so you come," said the guards.

Enes didn't want to go; he didn't believe in the exchange. They'd kill him, just like his mother.

"If your people agree to take you instead of your father, you'll go free," they said. "If not, you'll come back here."

*I'll never come back here*, he thought. *They'll kill me in the forest.*

He got on the bus. They drove out onto the main road from Banja Luka to Jajce.

They drove slowly.

They turned onto a field road, a track.

They went back to the highway. They drove on.

They stopped in the middle of the road.

The men were told to get out.

A few hundred yards further down the road there were some other people standing about.

A few of them started approaching, smiling and joking.

"As if they didn't know what was going on here," says Enes. "As if one side had brought peppers to market, and the other tomatoes."

The man in charge of the people who had come up to them—a Muslim—had a look at the prisoners.

"What have you done to them?" he asked the Serbian guards. "How much do they weigh? Forty-five pounds each? I'll give you your men—they weigh two hundred pounds each. You should be giving us three for each one."

It was a good joke, and everyone started laughing.

The Muslim went up to Enes.

"Where's your father?"

"He died in my arms," he replied as quietly as he could. "They beat him to death, smashed him up."

"These Chetniks killed your father?" repeated the other man in a loud voice. "Come with us."

Enes set off down the tarmac toward his own people. He wanted to run, but he could hardly walk. His legs were like stones; each step was like a mile, each second like a century. So he moved slowly but ever forward, without looking back.

"Now, with Dr. Klonowski's help, I'm identifying my brother's bones."

There will be a funeral, prayers, and a grave. Two graves, because his mother is here too: Sadeta, found with Mejra's daughter Edna.

## The First Lid, Then the Second

Now we are going inside the hall too. Mejra is leading the mourners along the wall, straight to a door on the left-hand side. In a small room, on the clean terracotta floor, two skeletons are lying side by side: Mejra's children.

"Ewa laid them out so beautifully here yesterday," says Mejra. "Ewa is lovely."

Uzeir is here too. He doesn't say anything.

Two white coffins are brought in, and some white sheets. The first lid goes on, then the second. The cortege now leaves from outside the hall and heads for Bosanski Petrovac, thirty miles away. That is where Mejra and Uzeir now live in a house that is not theirs but that used to be Serbian. "Our Mother Mejra has found her children!" People were still repeating the good news to each other there yesterday. Now they have gathered in large numbers outside the mosque to look at the coffins. Some (not all) go into the mosque to recite the Yasin Sura.

The cemetery is at Bihać, another thirty miles away. Here the following people join in: some former neighbors from Prijedor (like Mejra, they would like to know anything at all about their own relatives), Edna's girlfriends from college (young and pretty), the mothers of sons killed in

Bratunac and Srebrenica (like Mejra, they would like to hold a funeral)—and Dr. Ewa Klonowski is there too.

At the graveside the imam asks Allah to receive the deceased into his kingdom. A young woman goes up to the microphone. She speaks bravely and firmly: "Dear Edna! It is very hard to find the words to express our pain. The news that your body had been found revived cruel memories of Omarska, Trnopolje, and Keraterm. Those of us who were there will never forget, not for a single moment. There is no relief. We will fight to punish those who forced you to leave for your eternal home so young and so cruelly."

There are a funeral, prayers, and a grave. Two graves. "It's a great relief," says Mejra. "Everyone is invited back to our house."

Mother Mejra is exemplary. So says the imam. She has put her trust in Allah, and that gives her fortitude in her suffering. She knows that her children's births, deaths, and funerals were her destiny. She holds no grudge against God; she doesn't protest or blaspheme.

It is hard to understand that one person can do so much evil to another. People ask the imam: Why does God let it happen? Why did he desert us? It's a good thing they are asking, thinks the imam. In the old days, people in these parts never thought about God. They didn't need him for anything. Now we feel hatred toward our Serbian neighbors. The Koran teaches us that that is not allowed, and that we must forgive. It will be hard to do that—now we need God more than ever before. Only God can help us to overcome our hatred. But also our fear that this is not the end, that death at the hands of our neighbors will come back to haunt us. God alone can protect us and guide everyone here to forgiveness. Just as he is guiding Mejra.

Now, in the large room at Mejra and Uzeir's house, the imam is getting ready to recite the Yasin Sura, as the Koran commands. He will recite it in Arabic. Mejra takes a small tablecloth out of the cupboard and throws it purposefully across Ewa's knees. "Legs! Cover your legs!"

Does not man see that We have created him from the small seed? Then lo! he is an open disputant.

And he strikes out a likeness for Us and forgets his own creation. Says he: Who will give life to the bones when they are rotten?

Say: He will give life to them Who brought them into existence at first, and He is cognizant of all creation.

He Who has made for you the fire to burn from the green tree, so that with it you kindle fire.

Is not He Who created the heavens and the earth able to create the like of them? Yea! and He is the Creator of all, the Knower.

His command, when He intends anything, is only to say to it: Be, so it is.

Therefore glory be to Him in Whose hand is the kingdom of all things, and to Him you shall be brought back.

Mother Mejra is weeping with her eyes closed. The women bring roast lamb, salad, and, later, baklava from the kitchen.

It is becoming dark. Ewa is already in her car (she is driving to Sarajevo) and is talking to someone on her cell phone. She is talking about bones. Now she is ending the call. The phone rings again, and she smiles when she hears the voice of her daughter, who is celebrating her eighteenth birthday in Reykjavík. She wishes her daughter a happy birthday. Although it is raining, Ewa drives fast, speeding around corners. She takes another call. It is Mejra, saying, "I feel better now. Drive carefully."

2000–2002

*Funeral in Potočari, July 11, 2003*

## Chapter 11

# *Earth*

In the morning everyone thought it would be different from how it was then. That day the sun had been beating down without mercy, but today it's cold and it has been pouring since dawn. The cars, and hundreds of buses too, have flocked here in a long line. The Serb policemen, positioned along the road every hundred yards, have put on black capes and are on guard to make sure nothing happens to the people driving to Potočari.

We have come here for a huge funeral. It has stopped raining. Here, on July 11, 1995, more than twenty thousand people from Srebrenica sought refuge with the Dutch UN troops. They came from the neighboring town, which had bravely defended itself for three years, but that day it fell: the Serbs broke the siege and entered the town.

And today there are almost twenty thousand of us in Potočari. The sun is coming out.

That day the Dutch soldiers did not help the citizens of Srebrenica. The Serbs came to Potočari straight after them, surrounded the area, went in among the terrified people, took away the men, and pushed aside the women. The women were crying and the children were hiding in their arms.

Today some of those children are already grown up. They have come with their mothers from Sarajevo, Tuzla,

Mostar, Vienna, Frankfurt, Stockholm, and New York. They have baggy jeans, good shoes, hair gel, and digital cameras—they're going to film their mothers' suffering today. That day, exactly eight years ago, they waited in the fierce sunshine for hours on end with nothing to drink and no toilets, not knowing what would happen next. Now too the sun is shining more and more fiercely, the number of people is rising, and it's getting more and more crowded.

The Reis-Ulema, the most senior cleric among the Bosnian Muslims, calls upon Allah. Without God it would be hard to endure this event.

Finally the women and children were ordered onto buses or trucks—it happened right here, next to the trees. They were transported via Bratunac, Kravica, and Vlasenica, all the way to the front line, where they were told to go and join their own people.

But the teenage boys—all those taller than five feet—were detained in Potočari, and so were their elder brothers, fathers, and grandfathers. They too are here among us. They have come back. Or at least some of them: 282, each with a first name and a surname, in coffins.

The youngest was fourteen at the time.

The cemetery—a rectangle half a mile long and three hundred yards wide—has been built by the tarmac road, in the field where the Muslim men waited to die that day. By this road, which both the victims and their executioners had traveled for decades on their way to school, to work, or the disco in the nearby town. Recently a high fence was erected here with a wide gate, and a mosque was built—a light roof on pillars, with no walls—plots were marked out, paths were laid between them, and grass was sown. But only a few hundred graves have been dug, in the northern part of the cemetery. Most of the grass still waits untouched. And the people who are sitting on it now are waiting for their loved ones' bodies to be identified. They're watching with envy the people who already have graves.

That day the Serbs murdered at least seven thousand men here, and to this day exhumations of mass graves are still going on in the area. Identifying the remains has only picked up speed lately, since DNA laboratories were opened in Bosnia. Several thousand bodies have already been dug up and are waiting to be identified. There will be more funerals in Potočari.

On the northern side of the cemetery there are 282 open graves, each with a green board with the victim's name, a small coffin with no lid—according to tradition, the remains are placed on boards and covered in a green cloth—a heap of earth with some more boards on top of it to stop the earth from spilling onto the canvas, and seven spades; in a short while they'll be needed. The sun is blazing.

The Imam calls everyone to the front of the mosque, on the southern side of the cemetery. Today, as an exception, he allows the women to bow down before Allah along with the men—those women who have lost sons, husbands, and fathers here. The women who have had their heads bare are now tying on headscarves. The Reis-Ulema calls on the faithful to turn their desire for vengeance into reconciliation.

He calls on Europe to take care of truth and justice.

He calls on the world to make sure that never, nowhere and to no one should Srebrenica ever happen again.

Finally he calls on the mourners to return to the graves and bury their loved ones.

They're going to the northern side.

Quickly, as if they wanted to get this experience behind them. The heat is getting stronger and there's no shade anywhere.

The women are touching the coffins, stroking them, kissing and embracing them. They've got their men back here, where they were taken away from them.

The crowd is pushing; the graves are packed close together. The men are putting the coffins in the graves, but not every woman wants to let them. Someone screams—it's the mother of an eighteen-year-old who can't bear to part with her son. The men pry her off the coffin; her relatives take her in their arms and pour water on her face. The spades get moving.

The Serb policemen are watching this scene from behind the fence. They are on guard to make sure nothing bad happens to the Muslim mourners on Serb territory. More than just once or twice buses full of Muslim women have had stones thrown at them here. But today it's peaceful. No one wants to hurt anyone. The local Serbs have their own matters to attend to: they're fetching firewood from the forest for the winter, harvesting the crops, and cooking in their kitchens.

It'd be good to get away from here. For several minutes the earth has been hitting the boards. Seven spades above each of 282 graves; the dull thudding noise, multiplied, is getting louder and louder. The lamentation is becoming harder and harder to withstand for those who are still somehow holding out. Some are supporting others. The men are crying now too: those who are more than twenty years old are alive by some miracle—they must have emigrated from here before the war, and now they are thanking Allah for that.

We're not asking any questions.

July 11, 2003

# *Permissions*

The quotation from Tadeusz Mazowiecki is from an interview entitled "Order of the Emotions First Class," published in *Magazyn*, a supplement to *Gazeta Wyborcza*, no. 15 (475), April 11, 2002.